# The Best
*Stage Scenes*
# of 2001

**Smith and Kraus** *Books for Actors*

## YOUNG ACTOR SERIES

## SCENE STUDY SERIES

If you require prepublication information about upcoming Smith and Kraus books, you may receive our semiannual catalogue, free of charge, by sending your name and address to *Smith and Kraus Catalogue, PO Box 127, Lyme, NH 03768. Or call us at (800) 895-4331; fax: (603) 643-6431.*

# The Best
# *Stage Scenes*
# of 2001

edited by D. L. Lepidus

SCENE STUDY SERIES

A SMITH AND KRAUS BOOK

Published by Smith and Kraus, Inc.
177 Lyme Road, Hanover, NH 03755
www.SmithKraus.com

First Edition: July 2003
10 9 8 7 6 5 4 3 2 1

Cover illustration by Lisa Goldfinger
Cover design by Julia Hill Gignoux

The Scene Study Series 1067-3253
ISBN 1-57525-352-6

**NOTE: These scenes are intended to be used for audition and class study; permission is not required to use the material for those purposes. However, if there is a paid performance of any of the scenes included in this book, please refer to the permissions acknowledgment pages 204–210 to locate the source that can grant permission for public performance.**

# Contents

## Scenes for Women

## Scenes for Men

# Foreword

If you have purchased this book, or if you are thinking of purchasing this book, you are probably an acting student, a teacher of acting students, a professional actor, or working to become a professional actor. You are looking for material to work on in class, or to use for auditions. Hopefully, you have found Smith and Kraus's anthologies suited to your needs in the past. It is my hope, as the new editor of this series, that you will find this book even *more* useful.

Almost all the material in this book is from readily available published plays; so now, you will be able to read the whole play as you work on your role. In the case of material not from published plays, we have tried to include contact information for the author — or we will gladly refer any inquiry about getting the whole script directly to him or her.

Almost all the scenes in this book are about characters close to the actual age of the actors who will use this book — making the material easier for them to understand and use.

In closing, I would like to offer my profuse gratitude to Marisa Smith and Eric Kraus for entrusting me with the daunting but hugely rewarding task of editing this book. I would like to thank Elizabeth Monteleone for her kind assistance in procuring permissions to use the material herein. And I offer thanks, most especially, to all the playwrights and agents who graciously gave their permission to print these scenes from their wonderful plays.

— D. L. Lepidus

# Scenes for
# Men and Women

# The Book of Liz
## David and Amy Sedaris

*Comic*

Duncan (forties) and Elizabeth (thirties)

> *This is a farcical comedy about a "Squeamish" woman named Eliza-beth (the Squeamish are sort of like the Amish, only a lot funnier) who makes the most mouth-watering cheese balls you ever tasted. In a pique, Liz has left the Squeamish community and gone to work in a Cracker Barrel–type restaurant, Plymouth Crock. Duncan is a co-worker there. Elizabeth's probably in her thirties. He is probably a little older.*

> *Duncan enters carrying a shopping bag and a bouquet of helium bal-loons. He is off work and is dressed neatly but casually.*

DUNCAN: You're lucky, Liz, it took me forty-two years to get dry!

ELIZABETH: *(Laughs.)* Oh, Duncan.

DUNCAN: I think it's traditional to wait until *after* the procedure, but I thought I'd go ahead and give these to you now. *(He hands her the bag and the balloon bouquet.)*

ELIZABETH: Oh, you shouldn't have!

DUNCAN: There's a can of helium as well so you can perk 'em back up when they start getting lazy.

ELIZABETH: Then I'm going to keep them forever. Oh, look at these! Gosh it's good to see you.

DUNCAN: The folks at the Crock all pitched in. Well, all except for Donny. He says that store-bought gifts are just a lot of b.s. and that he's going to "make" you something.

ELIZABETH: I'm sure that whatever it is it will be lovely.

DUNCAN: I kept him on as a favor to some friends in the program, but I really think you should fire him, Liz. Just cut him loose. He's not a team player.

ELIZABETH: Well I'm not manager yet.

DUNCAN: At this point it's just a matter of getting you back on your feet and into your . . . ta da . . . *(He pulls out a catalog of restaurant uniforms.)* . . . new uniform!

ELIZABETH: A new uniform?

DUNCAN: Corporate headquarters took an opinion poll and it turns out that in the mind of John Q. Public, pilgrims are second only to the Italians when it comes to good cooking and nice big portions.

ELIZABETH: What's so great about Italians?

DUNCAN: Exactly! We think we can beat them, and I feel that we stand a pretty good chance. The problem is our image. When people think "pilgrim," they think stern and unforgiving.

ELIZABETH: That's so unfair.

DUNCAN: It might have been the case back in Colonial Jamestown, but as far as Plymouth Crock is concerned I happen to think we're a pretty fun group of people!

ELIZABETH: You've got my vote.

DUNCAN: It's our look that's turning people away. Too dark. Too heavy. So the folks upstairs have decided to lighten things up. The new uniforms will be a pancake, toasty sort of color . . . *(He hands her the catalog opened to the proper page.)*

ELIZABETH: You mean this one here, with the poncho and sombrero?

DUNCAN: No, silly, the one on top, worn over the turtleneck T-shirt. The guys, of course, will wear pants while the ladies will have a choice of either shorts or a skirt.

ELIZABETH: *(Holding up the catalog.)* You don't mean this skirt, do you? Why, it's no bigger than a bev nap.

DUNCAN: It's a little on the short side, but customers like to see a bit of leg. Studies prove it increases the appetite for bacon.

ELIZABETH: But Mr. T, I can't wear this.

DUNCAN: Sure you can, Liz. Have some confidence. I see a lot of women your age wearing this sort of thing.

ELIZABETH: It's not my age, I just . . . can't. The poncho, maybe, but the skirt or the shorts, no, they're out of the question.

DUNCAN: There's a special provision for the disabled, but as long as those are your real legs I'm afraid you're going to have to go along with the program. What is this, Liz, some sort of a . . . religious thing? You're not a Moslem, are you?

ELIZABETH: *(This is very hard for her to say.)* No I'm . . . I'm Squeamish. I'm from Cluster Haven, Duncan.

DUNCAN: *(Laughing.)* Right, like the folks in their buggies! Oh, that's a good one Liz.

ELIZABETH: Please don't act like that Duncan, not you.

DUNCAN: I'm sorry. But . . . Squeamish! From Cluster Haven? Why didn't you tell me?

ELIZABETH: No one ever asked and, seeing as it never got in the way of my job, I didn't see any reason to bring it up.

DUNCAN: Is that why you wear gloves when working the register? And ride the . . .

ELIZABETH: Llama to work. Yes. There are a lot of things I can work around, but a short skirt — it just goes against everything I believe in.

DUNCAN: Cluster Haven. That's a pretty big thing to withhold. I mean, a thing like that, it rules your life.

ELIZABETH: Well don't you start every shift with a group serenity prayer?

DUNCAN: That's different, Liz. I'm an alcoholic.

ELIZABETH: Great. So why don't you have a drink to celebrate your big promotion? Go out on the town with Conrad and treat yourself to a nice big bottle of Lancers.

DUNCAN: That's cruel, Liz. You know I can't have a drink. Especially Lancers.

ELIZABETH: And I can't wear a short skirt. It's the same thing, Duncan.

DUNCAN: Listen Liz, I can tell you right now that the guys upstairs are not going to accept anyone not wearing the new uniform. You'd be too much of a . . . loose cannon. I personally think you have what it takes but . . .

ELIZABETH: Ah, there's that *but* again. You people use that word a lot, Duncan. "We love you to death, *but* you sweat too much." "You'd make a great manager, *but* you won't wear a short skirt." "Your llama's really cute, *but* he can't have an employee parking space." *(She gets up from the chair and starts collecting her things.)*

DUNCAN: What are you doing?

ELIZABETH: Don't you see, Mister T? If I go through with this procedure there'll only be more buts. And I'll go along and go along until someone says, "We'd love to keep you on, *but* you're getting too old." And in the end I won't have anything left but a dry miniskirt and a plaque reminding me that once upon a time I was employee-of-the-month. I can face old age, Duncan, but not without my principles. Thanks for the offer, but I won't be needing the job. Or the leeches.

# The Book of Ruth
## Deborah Lynn Frockt

*Dramatic*

Ruth and David (teens)

> *David and Ruth are two teens in a concentration camp during World War II. David has found a "special place" in the camp in which he can fantasize about wonderful things — about being free. He shares its secret with Ruth.*

> *David and Ruth enter the secret place. Ruth is impressed.*

RUTH: How could you find this place?

DAVID: I told you I was good at things. Just not art things.

RUTH: Nobody knows of it but you?

DAVID: Not until now.

RUTH: It's so quiet.

DAVID: Private.

RUTH: Why didn't you keep this secret to yourself?

DAVID: I felt alone up here. Which was the idea — at first. To be alone. To breathe alone. But then it became too alone, and all I could think of was that there's no one down there for me and no one up here either — and it was too alone.

RUTH: Why did you pick me to tell?

DAVID: Maybe you're special.

RUTH: I'm not.

DAVID: You drew that picture.

RUTH: It was just something I thought of.

DAVID: If you can think it, it could be.

RUTH: Thinking something doesn't make it so.

DAVID: Yes it does. I wanted to find this place. I wanted to find a place where I didn't have to share every inch and suffocate every moment, and as I was thinking just that thought, I stopped and saw this building and I decided to go in. And I came five flights up to a floor that barely exists.

RUTH: It's high, isn't it? Probably higher than any place here.

DAVID: We're so close to your sky castle, we could smell the baking from here.

RUTH: There is no baking to smell.

DAVID: If we could smell it, we could taste it.

RUTH: What are you talking about?

DAVID: And if we tasted it, it would fill us. *(He closes his eyes.)* Close your eyes.

*(Ruth does not close her eyes. With his eyes still closed . . .)*

DAVID: Close your eyes.

*(Ruth closes her eyes.)*

DAVID: Now see if you can smell baking.

*(They sit in silence, straining to smell. Ruth opens her eyes.)*

RUTH: I don't smell anything.

DAVID: Then try harder. Think about your sky bakery.

*(Ruth closes her eyes. They strain to smell again. Ruth opens her eyes.)*

RUTH: I still don't smell anything — let alone fresh bread.

*(David reluctantly opens his eyes.)*

RUTH: It was just a picture.

DAVID: But we're in the sky.

RUTH: We're not in the sky. We're in a *kumbal.*

DAVID: We're in the sky.

RUTH: In a building.

DAVID: We're in the sky.

RUTH: In a fortress.

DAVID: We're in the sky.

RUTH: In the middle of a war.

DAVID: We're in the sky.

RUTH: You can make yourself believe that?

DAVID: It's true.

RUTH: All right. We're in the sky.

DAVID: So, if we're in the sky, all our sky needs is a bakery.

RUTH: A bakery?

DAVID: A bakery. We make a bakery.

RUTH: I suppose we'll just start by putting an oven up here.

DAVID: No. We'll have to make one.

RUTH: We just make an oven?

DAVID: Yes. We just make an oven.

RUTH: With what?

DAVID: Iron, steel.

RUTH: Iron and steel that you smuggled in past guards and thieves?

DAVID: Then rocks, stones, bricks, sticks. Whatever we can find. We'll
    make an oven, and in an oven we'll make bread. We'll make so much
    bread that there will be crumbs to give to the birds and extra to make
    a pudding and some even for tea.

RUTH: Bread?

DAVID: Fresh bread! If it began to look just a little stale, we'd throw the
    whole loaf out.

RUTH: Dark brown bread from Bohemia and fluffy white bread from Paris.

DAVID: Real bread.

RUTH: If there were real bread!

DAVID: There'd be real school.

RUTH: Real houses.

DAVID: Real games.

RUTH: Real rules.

DAVID: Real life. *(He picks up a stone.)* We've got work to do.

RUTH: You think we can do this?

DAVID: Are you hungry?

RUTH: Always.

DAVID: Then we don't have a choice. Now. How do you make an oven?

RUTH: I thought you'd know.

DAVID: I told you.

DAVID AND RUTH: I'm no good at art.

RUTH: Then I will be the oven architect.

DAVID: And I will be the oven architect assistant.

RUTH: We should start right here. *(She puts her foot down, but notices some-
    thing odd.)* This board is loose.

DAVID: Then do it here.

*(He moves here and Ruth gestures for him to lay the cornerstone. She straightens it slightly. David stands tall and begins to make a speech.)*

DAVID: Ahem . . . today marks the first day of our building. We hope to complete our oven quickly, so that we can begin baking without delay.

RUTH: Ahem . . . And when we bake, the bread will smell so sweet. Our noses and stomachs will be full of this bread, and we'll leave our rations far behind.

DAVID: This is *our* secret now. Both of ours.

*(David offers his hand to Ruth to seal the pact. They shake.)*

# The Butterfly Collection
## Theresa Rebeck

*Seriocomic*

Sophie (twenties) and Ethan (forties)

> *Sophie is an assistant to a famous but blocked novelist. Ethan is an actor.*
> *He is visiting his father, the novelist. He is married. He is very attracted*
> *to Sophie, and she to him, and in this scene they do something about it.*

> *Ethan sprawls on the couch for a long moment, thinking. Sophie enters,*
> *carrying the plate of butterflies. She sees him on the couch and turns to*
> *go back immediately.*

ETHAN: Hello.
*(Beat. Sophie stops, speaks with a polite innocence.)*
SOPHIE: I'm sorry. I thought you had gone. Margaret said you, all of you,
were going to lunch.
ETHAN: No, I decided not to go.
SOPHIE: Well. I'm glad you're here. I didn't mean to disturb you. But I
wanted to return the butterflies. I didn't realize how valuable they
were. I simply can't accept them.
ETHAN: You can't?
SOPHIE: No.
ETHAN: But you thought I was gone. So why bring the butterflies?
SOPHIE: I was going to leave them here. With a note.
ETHAN: Look. I'm sorry I put you in this position. It wasn't my inten-
tion. I —
SOPHIE: No, it's fine, I put myself there, I don't blame anyone, I just, it
can't happen again.
ETHAN: No.
SOPHIE: No.
ETHAN: I'm going back to the city tonight.

SOPHIE: Good. So, here are the butterflies and and — that's all.

ETHAN: Please, keep them.

SOPHIE: I can't keep them.

ETHAN: If you're worried about my girlfriend —

SOPHIE: I'm not worried about your girlfriend. Perhaps you should worry about your girlfriend; I don't know your girlfriend. The person *I* am worried about is . . .

*(She stops herself.)*

ETHAN: What?

SOPHIE: Nothing. Please. Just take them back. I need to go.

*(She starts to go.)*

ETHAN: He hit on you.

*(She turns and looks at him.)*

SOPHIE: What?

ETHAN: My father. Hit on you. Didn't he?

SOPHIE: *(A beat; surprised.)* Yes. He did.

ETHAN: What did you do?

SOPHIE: What did I *do?*

ETHAN: It's a fair enough question, Sophie. You're not as innocent as you pretend to be, and I suspect you've been hit on before.

SOPHIE: Never with such exquisite complication.

ETHAN: *(Angry.)* Are you going to tell me what happened or not?

SOPHIE: What do you think happened? He kissed me, and — it was — I, I am very confused right now, all right? So —

ETHAN: Did you enjoy it?

SOPHIE: *Enjoy* it? I don't — I was overwhelmed —

ETHAN: *(Overlap.)* Oh, overwhelmed. That's good. He over*whelmed* you. So you had nothing to do with it. It was rape, huh, you didn't enjoy it at all, you fought but you know, a sixty-four-year-old guy, he can be pretty over*whelm*ing —

SOPHIE: *(Angry.)* OK, "overwhelmed" was the wrong word. I was thrilled. It was thrilling —

ETHAN: *(Enraged.)* Thrilling. Which part, the kiss or the rest of it, was it thrilling to have my father feel you up?

*(She stares at him in shock. He backs down, turns away, knowing he's gone too far.)*

SOPHIE: Look. I am here to work. This is — I am here to write. I am here to learn.

ETHAN: An aging Nobel laureate and his demonic son have both fallen for you, simultaneously. If you can't learn from that, you're no writer.

SOPHIE: Yes, that's very amusing. Thank you.

ETHAN: Did you sleep with him?

SOPHIE: *(Biting.)* No! I didn't sleep with him!

ETHAN: Are you *going* to sleep with him?

*(She looks at him, enraged by this.)*

ETHAN: It's a fair question, Sophie. You came here —

SOPHIE: I came here to *work* —

ETHAN: Well, other things happened, didn't they? What, am I just his son? Is that all I am to you, "his son," you made a mistake, you slept with the son when you could have had the man himself! Sold yourself short, didn't you? Got to get rid of the son now, 'cause Dad's the real prize!

SOPHIE: That is not what I am doing!

ETHAN: It is exactly what you're doing!

SOPHIE: You're leaving anyway, you just said —

ETHAN: Well, that explains your relief. I'm taking off, so you and dad have a clear playing field.

SOPHIE: This is impossible. You see? You must see how impossible this is, already — this entire week has been a nightmare, going in there ten hours a day after I turned him down, believe me, is no fucking picnic, but I do it! And I intend to continue doing it, so I cannot do *this!*

*(She starts for the door.)*

ETHAN: So you're doing this for your *art, that's* why you've been dodging me all week?

SOPHIE: I'm trying to survive here!

ETHAN: It's going to save you, isn't it? Make you whole. Make you wise. A really great sentence, shows you a corner of insight into the human condition, you think you've seen the face of god. That's why Paul has you. Got to get close to that, he's the lodestone, the magic, you have to touch it, like the hem of Christ's robe — *(Beat.)* It's OK. He's got me, too. All that art, all that approval, all that love, just out of reach. The big hole inside you, he's the only thing that can plug that up. And he's a complete shithead.

SOPHIE: I should have done it. Is that what you're saying?

ETHAN: Quite the opposite, Sophie. I think you know that.

*(Beat.)*

SOPHIE: I am drowning here.

ETHAN: I have to know this. If it were just me. If it were you, and me, and nothing else. No one else. What would you be saying to me now?

SOPHIE: *(Lost.)* It's not possible to do that.

ETHAN: It is. He is not here. I am the only one here.

*(He is close to her. They kiss. The kiss begins to get involved, but she pulls away.)*

SOPHIE: We can't do this here.

*(She takes him out. Blackout.)*

# Buying Time
## Michael Weller

*Dramatic*

Ben (forties) and Christine (thirties)

> *Ben is a partner in a law firm, married with two children. Chris is an environmental activist. In this scene, he comes to Chris's apartment. She thinks he's interested in an important case involving them both; while, in fact, he's interested in her.*

> *A 1930s bungalow. Southwest Native-American craftwork in a Spartan decor. Chris, in khaki shorts and net tank top — it's a hot evening, leads Ben in. He's in a rumpled jacket and oxford shirt. He looks tired.*

CHRIS: You were driving by, my light was on, it's ten PM — ?

BEN: *(Raising his briefcase in explanation.)* An old case of mine, *Spotted Owl vs. Oregon Timber.* I won, slam dunk. You can plug in Grayhawk and everything tracks.

CHRIS: A Greek bearing gifts. Does this mean bad news? Let me guess, you won't supervise?

BEN: *(Pause.)* Carter blew it. His interview made Grayhawk glow in the dark. The bad guys'll be watching it like Monday Night Football.

CHRIS: *(Q.E.D.)* If you'd been counseling us —

BEN: Are you and Carter an item? Is he trying to impress you?

CHRIS: He's trying to get your firm's attention. *And* stop the road. Looks like he hit a double bull's-eye.

BEN: He hit a hornet's nest, and my firm's going to get stung.

CHRIS: Could you be more specific?

BEN: No.

CHRIS: *(Pause.)* Would bad red wine make a difference? Or slightly better Scotch?

BEN: No. Thank you. *(Carefully.)* Look, Ms. Martel, there's a rift within

D&R of long standing — and of a nature which might behoove a client like LivEarth to seek alternate counsel.

CHRIS: Max took this case five months ago. Now suddenly we're poison because of one little item in the newspaper?

BEN: "Little?!" Centerfold feature; child clutching dead Grayhawk? Reinhardt headquarters with skull and crossbones superimposed — ?

CHRIS: *(Interrupting.)* Are you dropping us?

BEN: *(Utterly miserable.)* That drink — is it still available?

CHRIS: No; I mean, first tell me what's so urgent it takes a visit at ten PM?

BEN: *(Beat.)* Our firm has a bylaw about pro bono —

CHRIS: Rule 7: "Partners may use 20 percent of their billable hours for public interest work with full pay and bonus entitlement."

BEN: That's right, you know everything about us, don't you?

CHRIS: It's a legend in the legal world; rob from corporate to fight for the meek.

BEN: This attitude thing, is it to prove you're hip and worldly-wise, 'cause I find it incredibly irritating.

CHRIS: I'm just protecting myself.

BEN: From what?

CHRIS: Whatever you're having so much trouble telling me; it feels ominous.

BEN: Well guess what, this is hard for me, too . . . trying to explain why my firm, a firm I'm very proud of — might be at a moment where we're compelled to act in a way — I'm not very proud of.

CHRIS: Why should I consider alternate counsel, Mr. Traube?

BEN: Because . . . this is a bad time for idealists. We have to pick our battles with care.

CHRIS: *(Pointed.)* Why should I consider alternate counsel?

BEN: We may be compelled to please certain clients at the expense of others. I really can't say any more. *(Beat.)* I shouldn't even be here, I better go.

CHRIS: Scotch, was it?

*(She pours. Bennett steals a glance at his watch; seeing this:)*

CHRIS: You have one of those watches that tells you the next move?

BEN: Without ice. *(Beat.)* You live alone? Witty repartee.

CHRIS: *(Pouring his drink.)* I'm *not* an idealist, Mr. Traube. I need access, not protection.

BEN: Bennett. Please.

CHRIS: I want Reinhardt for personal reasons. Irrational, even. Which is usually why we do things, don't you think?

BEN: Odd view for a lawyer.

CHRIS: To beat Reinhardt you need something crazy driving you; as crazy as whatever's driving him; arrogance, presumption, greed — I don't know, what is it that lets one man destroy irreplaceable things in the world then sleep through the night? We'll fight by the rules, of course; courtroom, judge, all that civilized stuff. But just under the skin it's a state of nature, and the maddest blood always wins — always.

BEN: Is that your legal theory for the case?

CHRIS: I had this uncle, Granger — a park ranger he was . . .

BEN: Granger the Ranger?

CHRIS: *(Smiles acknowledgement.)* He'd go on these benders and pass out for days. I rode his horse into the woods, and I'd wear a blindfold. It was a game; no, a challenge. I had to wind up somewhere I wouldn't recognize when I took the blindfold off, then let my horse go and find my way home, only a knife and matches allowed. And the trick was to never let fear in. One time I was out five days. I fell asleep thinking, "Tonight I'll die, and animals will eat me. I'll vanish without a trace." *(Smiles at herself.)* I was a dramatic child.

BEN: How'd you get home?

CHRIS: You're missing the point. I'm talking about fear, how you master it. How I learned not to be afraid, ever. That forest became mine in the end: my wild place.

BEN: *(Beat.)* Is there some reason you're telling me this?

CHRIS: Reinhardt cut it down years ago. Ranger lost his job, drank himself to death. End of story.

BEN: So this is revenge.

CHRIS: *(Focused.)* The Tuintu's a lot like that forest. Ponderosa Pine: a very powerful tree. Reinhardt wants to cut down another wild place like the one where I was happy once. So, I'm going to destroy him.

BEN: Well. *(What can he say.)* Good luck.

CHRIS: Are you not listening, or don't you take me seriously.

BEN: *(Suddenly.)* I came here to make love.

CHRIS: Oh.

# Comic Potential
## Alan Ayckbourn

*Comic*

Adam and Jacie (twenties to thirties)

> *Adam is an aspiring writer visiting the set of a TV soap opera. The actors are all robots ("actoids"). In this scene, he meets JC-31-333, Jacie, the actoid who plays the Nurse. Jacie is about Adam's age, and her programming has developed a flaw: She can think creatively and she can feel emotion.*

> *Behind Adam, quite suddenly, the Nurse laughs.*

ADAM: *(Jumping in alarm.)* Oh, my God. You're alive? What am I going — ? You're live! Are you supposed to be live?

NURSE: I'm active, yes.

ADAM: Well, are you supposed to be? Should I be unplugging you or something? I was supposed to unplug you if you whistled.

NURSE: Then I promise not to whistle. *(Looking at the screen.)* Who is this?

ADAM: This is one of the greatest silent comedians the world has ever known. His name was Buster Keaton. Have you heard of him?

NURSE: No.

ADAM: He ran his own studios for a time, way back in the early 1920s. Silent comedy. You know? Comedy without words.

NURSE: No words?

ADAM: Keaton broke new ground because — Excuse me. Are we conversing?

NURSE: Yes, I think so. I'm listening. You're talking.

ADAM: Yes. Is that — ? I mean, you are a — an — aren't you?

NURSE: An actoid, yes.

ADAM: And you talk?

NURSE: Oh, yes. An actoid needs to talk. Unless they're Buster Keaton. *(She smiles. Adam smiles back.)*

ADAM: This is ridiculous.

NURSE: Why?

ADAM: I don't know. I just didn't expect to be having a conversation. Do you always talk to people like this?

NURSE: No. Normally people don't converse. It's quicker to direct-link through the computer.

ADAM: Then why now? Why me?

NURSE: Because you're talking to me.

ADAM: And do you have a name? I mean . . .

NURSE: Oh, yes. My name is currently Bridget Bonny. Nurse Bridget Bonny.

ADAM: No, that's the name of your character, surely?

NURSE: That's right. *(Slightly Yorkshire.)* I'm twenty-four years old and I was born in Halifax, Yorkshire, but at a very early age my parents moved south to —

ADAM: But what's your real name?

NURSE: *(A little puzzled.)* My real name?

ADAM: Your real name. You must have a real name?

NURSE: Oh, yes, I see. The name I was made with. It is JC — F31 — triple 3.

ADAM: Jacie? Pretty. May I call you Jacie?

JACIE: If you wish.

ADAM: I'm Adam.

JACIE: Yes, I heard.

ADAM: Tell me, Jacie. I'm interested. What made you laugh, during the filming? At the end there?

JACIE: I don't know.

ADAM: Did you find it funny?

JACIE: Yes. I'm afraid I have a fault.

ADAM: Not necessarily. Just because you laugh doesn't mean you have a fault.

JACIE: It just happened. I had no control.

ADAM: No, that's natural. We see something funny, we laugh. Involuntarily, sometimes. We can't help ourselves.

JACIE: I think I have a fault.

ADAM: You found Keaton funny, too?

JACIE: Oh, yes. In a different way. That little look he gave.

ADAM: The look? Oh, you mean the take?

JACIE: Take?

ADAM: The double take. You know about double takes?

JACIE: No.

ADAM: It's a well-known comic device — the double take — or in Keaton's case the quarter take. The demi semi minuscule take. But at the other end of the scale you have someone like — let's see — James Finlayson — Finlayson's a good example. He was famous from the Laurel and Hardy movies. Do you know the — ? No? Well, Finlayson would do takes where he literally took off and left the ground. Bold massive takes. Like this.

*(He demonstrates badly. Jacie looks puzzled.)*

Really funny. When he did them. Do you need to stay plugged in?

JACIE: Yes.

ADAM: OK, stay sitting down, I'll teach you. Right. Let's see. Imagine you're reading a book, yes?

JACIE: I'm reading a book.

ADAM: You hear me come into the room . . . You know it's me, so you don't look up at once. What you don't know is that I am covered in mud. I have fallen in a puddle outside the house and I am covered in black slimy mud from head to toe. You look up casually, you see me, register my presence but your book is so interesting you go quickly back to it. You do that . . .

*(Jacie does so.)*

ADAM: Now, as you look at your book again, the image of me suddenly registers on your brain. You realize what you've seen. You look at me again. Quickly, sharply this time. Amazed.

*(Jacie does so.)*

ADAM: All right. Let's do the whole thing. You're reading your book. Here I come. Covered in mud.

*(Adam clumps rather heavily into the room. Jacie glances at him, then back at her book.)*

JACIE: Hallo, dear, is it raining?

*(She does the rest of the take.)*

ADAM: *(Impressed.)* Good! Excellent. Your first double take.

JACIE: Was it all right for me to put in the line?

ADAM: Er . . . yes. Yes, that was fine. It wasn't strictly necessary but it was fine. Good. We'll make a comedian of you yet. *(They smile at each other. Adam executes a rather clumsy comic trip.)* Whoops!
*(Jacie frowns.)*

ADAM: Next week, the custard pie.

JACIE: The custard pie? Is that funny?

ADAM: In the right hands. It's a — it's basically just a pie. Full of custard— or usually cream. Flat on a plate. And when someone annoys you — or gets up your nose — you know — you take the pie and you squash it in their face and you twist it — like that — so it —

JACIE: — oes up their nose —

ADAM: You got it.

JACIE: That's funny?

ADAM: Er — not to talk about, no. It's a visual gag.

JACIE: Custard pie . . . *(She copies his mime.)* Yes, that could be funny. *(She smiles at him and laughs. He smiles and laughs, too. They stare at each other. Adam looks away, rather embarrassed suddenly. The lights fade.)*

# Comic Potential
## Alan Ayckbourn

*Comic*

Adam and Jacie (twenties to thirties)

> *Adam is an aspiring TV writer. He has met Jacie on the set of a TV soap opera. Jacie is an "actoid" — a robot actress. Her programming has developed a flaw: she can think creatively and feel emotion. Adam is in love with her and determined to create a TV series featuring her. The two have run off together and are here in a friend's apartment (Chandler).*

ADAM: *(He looks at the bottle of Scotch. He picks it up, opens Chandler's drawer again, and fishes out a glass. He is about to pour himself one.)* Would you like one? Or —

JACIE: Sure. A man should never drink alone.

ADAM: Right. *(Finding another glass.)* I just had a thought. Why should you need a drink?

JACIE: I drink.

ADAM: Yes?

JACIE: And I eat.

ADAM: You do?

JACIE: The sort of shows I do, we're required to eat and drink a lot.

ADAM: Yes.

JACIE: They're all eating and drinking.

ADAM: Really. Cheers.

JACIE: Cheers.

ADAM: Does the nurse eat? I mean your character as the nurse?

JACIE: No, Bridget drinks. She's a secret alcoholic.

ADAM: Is she?

JACIE: That's why I gave her the laugh, you know. With the doctor. I thought she could be drunk on duty.

ADAM: *(Laughing.)* Whose idea was that? To make her an alcoholic.

JACIE: Mine. She was very boring otherwise. She just stood and nodded a lot.

ADAM: I see. *(Pause.)* How do you — this is a personal question, you don't have to answer it if you find it too personal — but what happens to all the food and the drink when you've finished with it? If you see what I mean?

JACIE: Someone comes along and empties me.

ADAM: Stupid question. Obviously. *(Pause.)* What did he mean by melt you down? What did he mean?

JACIE: Melt down? That's when you're returned to the factory and they erase your memory and then reboot with the basic program. I would be like Jacie in your play if that happened. I would start again.

ADAM: *(Sipping his whiskey.)* Hey, this is strong. *(He coughs.)* More?

JACIE: Keep 'em coming, kid.

ADAM: *(Laughing.)* And what show does that come out of? Keep 'em coming, kid? Honestly!

JACIE: Episode nineteen, scene four, line twelve of *Some Dark Alley.* I was an undercover policewoman. Josie. She was shot. It was a good death scene. *(Instantly in the scene, in great pain.)* "Help me, Jason, help me. You mean more to me than I've ever been able to — tell — you . . . I'm sorry . . ." It was a good scene.

ADAM: I don't want you melted down. I think that would be criminal.

JACIE: No. No crime. Not for an actoid.

ADAM: All your memory gone. All you are. Wouldn't that upset you?

JACIE: I've nothing I care to remember. Well, the last few days maybe.

ADAM: That's terribly sad. It makes me feel like crying. You wouldn't mind if Jacie — the person you are now — just ceased to exist?

JACIE: I'd never know, would I? How could I mind? *(She reaches out and gently strokes his head. Softly.)* Cry if you want to.

*(He looks up at her. A moment between them, then he moves away.)*

ADAM: No, sitting here feeling sorry for myself is not the way. Come on, let's — I don't know. What shall we do? Go out and eat? No, that'd be no fun for you, would it? What do you want to do?

JACIE: Dance.

ADAM: Dance?

JACIE: I want to dance. I never get to dance.

ADAM: All right. If that's what you want. Music? How do we get music, do you know?

JACIE: In that drawer. There's his collection of disks.

*(Adam opens a drawer.)*

ADAM: Hey, yes! Wow! Another treasure trove. These you have loved. I'm not a good dancer. I have to warn you. Are you a good dancer?

JACIE: Yes. I have a program.

ADAM: I somehow thought you would. Now, what's this? Zed Zed Top? Who are they? Let's try Zed Zed Top, then. *(He puts the disk into the panel. The sound of ZZ Top's "My Head's in Mississippi" booms out.)* Yes? What about this?

JACIE: It's good. It's funny.

*(She begins to move. Gently at first. Adam joins her.)*

ADAM: Hey, you do dance, don't you?

JACIE: I dance.

*(It is apparent from the start that she is going to run rings around him, but he keeps it up gamely for a bit until her program kicks into gear and she goes into overdrive. At the finish, Adam is left sitting breathless watching her admiringly.)*

JACIE: I'm sorry. Are you all right?

ADAM: *(Breathless still.)* God, you're beautiful. You're so beautiful.

*(She smiles and offers him her hand. She helps him to his feet. We get some idea of her strength from the effortless way she does this. They stand holding each other for a second. Adam kisses her gently. She responds. Music starts again, this time from Jacie. Very romantic. A love theme.)*

ADAM: Is that you?

JACIE: Yes, I'm sorry. Shall I stop it?

ADAM: No. It's fine. It goes with the scene.

*(They dance a little, gently this time.)*

JACIE: Adam, I don't want to be melted down. I don't want to forget this.

ADAM: Nobody's going to melt you down, I promise.

JACIE: Promise?

ADAM: I promise.

JACIE: Oh, Adam . . .

ADAM: Jacie . . .

JACIE: Adam . . .

*(The music continues as the lights fade to blackout.)*

# Comic Potential
## Alan Ayckbourn

*Comic*

Adam and Jacie (twenties to thirties)

> *Adam is an aspiring writer in love with Jacie, who is a robot, an "ac-toid" on a TV soap opera. They are on the lam and are hiding out here in a very seedy hotel.*

> *The hotel bedroom. Adam and Jacie enter.*

ADAM: We'll be safe up here as long as we stay in the room. We'll have to keep out of the public areas till I find us another hotel. Somewhere less conspicuous. Less — particular.

JACIE: What's a trollop?

ADAM: Have they got a phone book in here somewhere? What is a what?

JACIE: A trollop?

ADAM: A trollop? It's an old-fashioned word. It means a whore. A prostitute.

JACIE: Oh.

ADAM: *(Still hunting for the phone book.)* They must have one somewhere. Why do you ask?

JACIE: No reason.

> *(Adam hunts about.)*

JACIE: How do you think the press found out?

ADAM: How do you think? *(Finding the phone book.)* Ah!

JACIE: Mrs. Pepperbloom?

ADAM: Almost certainly. Now then . . . Hotels? *(He starts to scan the book.)*

JACIE: Adam?

ADAM: Mmm?

JACIE: Are we staying the night here?

ADAM: Yes, just tonight. We should be safe for one night.

JACIE: May I try on my things?

ADAM: What things?

JACIE: You know my — new surprise things?

ADAM: *(Distracted.)* Yes, sure. Go ahead. Ah. Hotel Mombassa. That sounds a possible.

*(He starts to dial. Jacie goes into the bathroom.)*

ADAM: *(Calling to her.)* This will only be temporary. Until we can work out something more permanent. I think if I can talk to uncle on my own, I could persuade him to change his mind. If not, I'm going to do a deal with him to rent you for long enough to make the movie elsewhere. There are plenty of other producers, for God's sake. *(Into phone.)* Hallo. Have you a double room for tomorrow night? . . . No, all night . . . yes . . . that's OK. The name is — Merryweather . . . M - E - R - no, R . . . R for rabbit . . . R . . . could you make that Jones. Yes. Mr. and Mrs. Jones. All night. Yes. 'Bye. *(Calling to Jacie.)* Sounds wonderful on the phone. *(Adam rises and paces the room as he talks.)* Listen, I've been thinking. You really should learn to read, you now. You see, if we do have to go completely independent on this — and I'm prepared to — I'm fully prepared to — then we may have to do it without a great deal of backup, technical backup.

*(Jacie has re-entered from the bathroom. She is wearing a new night-dress she has bought from the shop. She stands posed, waiting for him to see her. He is so engrossed he barely notices.)*

ADAM: No programers. You'll have to work completely hands free. No direct feed at all. Do it the old-fashioned way. Looking at the script, learning it or at least scanning it in advance and then interpreting it entirely for yourself. I know you're capable of that. I have total faith in your talent, Jacie. All we need is a good, supportive director for you. Give you the confidence. Someone who can bring out the best in you. Who you'd feel comfortable working with.

*(Jacie has gone back into the bathroom again.)*

ADAM: If we could get Chance, of course, that would be just wonderful. But there are others, nearly as good. Don't worry — where have you gone? — because all I'm saying is that in the end it's got to be your show, Jacie. It's going to succeed or fail on your personality. I do have some money. Enough certainly to set this up in a modest way. I mean, not a fortune but we don't have to go mad. I can simplify it all down. Reduce the number of locations. Rent a small studio somewhere. *(Jacie returns. She is now wearing a coat.)*

ADAM: What I think we — *(Noticing her for the first time.)* What are you doing?

JACIE: *(Grimly.)* Nothing. *(She starts to open and shut the drawers.)*

ADAM: I thought you were getting ready for bed?

JACIE: I don't need sleep. I'll just plug into the socket in the corner there and recharge. I won't bother you. I just make a faint buzzing.

ADAM: Don't you want to show me your surprise?

JACIE: *(Finding a Gideon Bible in one of the drawers.)* I tried it. I looked like a trollop. Here. *(She hands him the Bible.)*

ADAM: What's this?

JACIE: A book. To read. You can teach me to read. It can fill in the time.

ADAM: What's the matter with you?

JACIE: Nothing. I want to learn to read, please. Teach me that book.

ADAM: This is a Bible.

JACIE: I understand that's a very good book.

ADAM: It's a very long book —

JACIE: Please. I want to be right for you. I don't want to spoil your play. Teach me to read. I promise, I'm quick. I learn fast.

ADAM: Well, all right, if that's what you . . . Come and sit here. I'll show you.

*(They sit together on the bed side by side. Adam opens the Bible at the beginning.)*

ADAM: Right. You understand the general principle of reading? All these different little clumps are words, do you see?

JACIE: Yes.

ADAM: And every word is made up of letters. And there are only twenty-six letters to remember but they make up hundreds of different words. Thousands and thousands of words. Look at this. This is an I, you see. Then that is an N and those two together make the word *in,* you see?

JACIE: IN . . .

ADAM: Next word, T - H - E — that makes THE, you see? So we get IN

THE. Now here's a big word B - E - G - that makes BEG or B'G, in this case, because then we get —

JACIE: IN

ADAM: Good.

JACIE: IN — IN.

ADAM: No, ING. That was a G on the end, you see?

JACIE: IN THE BEG — INN — ING . . . BEGINNING . . .

ADAM: Good! Then here's a G again which we know, but then here's a new letter O, that's an O and then a D. Those three make GOD.

JACIE: GOD. IN THE BEGINNING GOD . . .

ADAM: Here we go, more new letters. That's a C — then an R — E, we've had before — A, that's an A, then a T. You see that's a T again?

JACIE: T.

ADAM: Then another E there and then D again. And that makes CRE-ATED.

JACIE: CREATED.

ADAM: Then what's the next word?

JACIE: THE

ADAM: Good. CREATED THE — ? Now we know these letters — H — that's an H —

JACIE: E — A —

ADAM: Good. New one. V, that's a V — that makes HEAV — ?

JACIE: EN — HEAVEN.

ADAM: Good.

JACIE: AND THE *(Struggling with the word.)* Ear — Eart — Ear — tuh — huh

ADAM: No, that's EARTH.

JACIE: IN THE BEGINNING GOD CREATED THE HEAVEN AND THE EARTH —

ADAM: That is very good. That's impressive.

JACIE: *(Struggling on.)* AND THE EARTH . . . ?

ADAM: W — AS —

JACIE: WA — WAS WITH — OUT —

ADAM: That's an F. A Fuh. Fuh — ORM.

JACIE: AND THE EARTH WAS WITHOUT FORM AND — *(She hesitates again.)*

ADAM: VOID. Those two together go OY.

JACIE: FORM AND VOID. And DAR —

ADAM: K, that's a K. DARK — NESS. Those are S's. Like Snakes. Sss.

JACIE: NESS — DARKNESS WAS uh —

ADAM: UPON. That one's a P. Makes a Puh sound.

JACIE: . . . UPON THE FACE OF THE DEEP . . . AND THE SPIRIT OF GOD MOVED UPON THE FACE OF THE WATERS —

ADAM: Very good.

JACIE: AND GOD SAID —

ADAM: L — that's an L. Luh. L — ET

JACIE: LET THERE BE — *(She frowns.)*

ADAM: LIGHT —

JACIE: LIGHT . . . AND THERE WAS LIGHT. And there was light. *(She smiles.)* And there was light. How beautiful. I'm longing to know what happens. *(Continuing to read rapidly.)* And God saw the light, that it was good; and God divided —

ADAM: Hang on! Hang on! That's enough for one night. *(Taking the Bible from her gently.)* First things first, please.
*(She looks at him. He kisses her gently. She smiles. He smiles at her. Her music starts.)*

JACIE: Do you mind the music? I couldn't help it.

ADAM: No. It's always good to know how people feel. *(He goes to kiss her again.)*

JACIE: *(Drawing back momentarily.)* Adam, I need to tell you, I am only constructed for simulated sex.

ADAM: Yes, I gathered that in the restaurant when I was under the . . . I'm sorry, I didn't mean to pry, I just couldn't help noticing.

JACIE: They did warn me. Once a man's seen your trap door, he loses all respect for you.

ADAM: *(Smiling.)* That's very funny. Where did that come from?

JACIE: *(Puzzled.)* I don't remember.
*(He kisses her.)*

JACIE: Adam, you'll tell me if I'm a trollop, won't you?

ADAM: I most certainly will. I never kiss trollops on principle.

# The Credeaux Canvas
## Keith Bunin

*Dramatic*

Winston (twenties) and Amelia (twenties)

> *Winston is an art student and gifted art forger. Amelia was his room-*
> *mate's girlfriend, whom he painted nude and then had sex with. In this*
> *scene, the final one in the play, Amelia returns to Winston's apartment*
> *to see Winston, whom she hasn't seen in a while, and to see his paint-*
> *ing of her one more time.*
>
> *Amelia stands with her back to us; she turns She is dressed in a purple*
> *cashmere sweater and gray slacks. Heels. Lovely but not overly opulent*
> *jewelry. A tasteful amount of base and blush. Her hair is ornately pinned*
> *up. She considers her surroundings very closely, as if she does not want*
> *to let any detail escape her notice. Winston emerges from the bathroom*
> *holding a glass of water. He wears glasses now and a pair of paint-*
> *spattered sweatpants.*

AMELIA: I forgot that you don't have a kitchen sink.

WINSTON: It's rustic living, but, um, I like it. *(He hands her the glass of water.)*

AMELIA: For the life of me I did not expect to find you here. I thought, I've got a couple hours before I have to catch the train back to Connecticut, I should visit all my old haunts, I saw your name on the buzzer, I nearly jumped out of my skin. I can't believe you're still living in this place.

WINSTON: I really hate, you know, moving. *(Attempting conviviality.)* So, what brings you to the city?

AMELIA: I spent the day uptown at the Jean-Paul Credeaux exhibit.

WINSTON: No kidding.

AMELIA: You've seen it, of course.

WINSTON: Yeah, um, a few months ago, when it opened.

AMELIA: What a madhouse. Lines around the block. Well, you predicted it. And it only took four years.

WINSTON: Four years? Really? Boy, time sure flies when you're, um, not paying attention.

AMELIA: And me, squeezing my way through the turnstiles, past the middle-aged couples from Passaic and the German families on holiday and the old ladies in their sensible shoes killing time before the matinee. I couldn't believe what a tourist I've become. I spent so many years trying to make this place my home, and now look at me, I am truly a stranger in this town.

WINSTON: *(A moment, then:)* I thought about calling you, you know, when Jamie died.

AMELIA: *(As neutral as possible.)* That would've been nice.

WINSTON: I wasn't even sure, um, you knew it had happened.

AMELIA: His stepmother wrote me. Remember her? Gail? A lovely note. I was awfully touched that she — I mean, I only met her once, I wasn't even aware that I had entered her mind. *(Looks down, her voice low.)* One thing I was sort of morbidly curious about, she didn't tell me *how* he — I don't know why, but that seems important to know.

WINSTON: *(Squirming a little.)* Oh. Well. He, uh, swallowed a bottle of pills. In a girl's apartment, on Chrystie Street, I think. I didn't get the details, either.

AMELIA: You weren't in touch with him, then?

WINSTON: *(Shakes his head.)* I hadn't seen him in, what, six months at least. Actually the last day I saw him was, you know, the last day I saw you. *(A beat.)* I looked for you at the funeral.

AMELIA: *(Smiles sadly.)* I didn't hear about it in time. I don't think I could've gone anyway. It would've been kind of a travesty for me to be there, don't you think?

WINSTON: That's the reason I wanted to call you, um, I was really afraid you would take it on yourself, what happened to Jamie. But he had always been so unhappy, you know, his mom dying when he was so young, and then his dad and all, plus there was probably so much more going on that, um, we never even knew about.

AMELIA: *(Stares at him evenly.)* That's a comforting thing to say, but sometimes I wake up in the middle of the night in a cold sweat and I lie in the tub shivering till dawn, or I walk across the playground and I start shaking all over and I have to sit in my car till it passes. And then I have to admit that in the end he did it entirely because of me. It was you and me.

WINSTON: *(Deeply uncomfortable.)* So, um, what have you been doing with yourself in Connecticut?

AMELIA: Past three years I've been the chorus teacher at Ridgefield Elementary School.

WINSTON: Wow, um, that must be fun, I guess. And I noticed, um, a wedding ring.

AMELIA: Would you believe the gym teacher?

WINSTON: No way. Kids too?

AMELIA: *(Nods.)* Twins. Jack and Sarah. Gabe took them on an outing in the country today. A petting zoo. Which he's happy to do, because believe me, he'd rather swallow glass than waste his Sunday at a museum. Not even to look at paintings of naked ladies. I have photos of everybody in my wallet but I won't bore you.

WINSTON: No, um, I'd really like to see.

AMELIA: *(Flashes him a bright smile.)* Actually I'm not sure I want to show you anything.

WINSTON: *(A moment, then, raises his hands.)* Oh. OK. Fine. Whatever. *(A pause.)* It seems like, um, you're really happy.

AMELIA: Oh, sure. I mean, there are moments, particularly when they're getting especially cranky in their car seats, or when Gabe pitches a fit because I threw his favorite sweats in the laundry or something asinine like that. And then it's like I can *feel* the life draining out of me. But then I'm putting them to bed, and Gabe is dozing in front of the TV, and the house is so peaceful, and I have this tremendous sense of . . . relief.

WINSTON: That sounds, you know, very nice.

AMELIA: And what about you? Is there anyone important in your life?

WINSTON: *(Stuffs his hands in his pockets.)* No. There's no one important in my life.

AMELIA: We get the Sunday *Times* so Gabe can do the crossword, I always flip through the Arts and Leisure section looking for your name.

WINSTON: Oh, well, that would be kind of, um, a fool's errand.

AMELIA: How have things been going?

*(Distractedly Winston sharpens his pencils with his paring knife.)*

WINSTON: I cart my portfolio around. But everybody's pretty much already seen me. The consensus is my stuff is too remote and technical, it feels more like, um, an exercise than an expression, I'm too derivative and far too, you know, self-consciously imitative.

AMELIA: But you're still painting every day.

WINSTON: *(Extends his arms helplessly.)* What else am I going to do?

AMELIA: *(A moment, then, nods.)* Well. I admire your persistence.

WINSTON: There was one flurry of activity a while back. Do you remember that awful day — Tess Anderson Rose actually bought one of my paintings. When she died, Christie's auctioned off her entire collection. So there was a week when I got about a hundred phone calls from the auction house, I had to fax them my bio for the catalogue, it was all, you know, pretty entertaining.

AMELIA: Did your painting fetch a good price?

WINSTON: *(Shakes his head.)* They couldn't give it away. But the Jean-Paul Credeaux still life she owned, that went for three and a half million dollars.

AMELIA: I saw it in the exhibit. It's really a wonderful painting, isn't it? And the portraits of those prostitutes — my God! I didn't understand them when you showed me the pictures in the magazine, but to see them up close — those women! One of them is barely twelve years old, one of them you can tell she's going to be dead within a week, but they're all just sitting there bathed in this extraordinary, thick kind of light.

WINSTON: I know, it's, um, amazing, isn't it?

AMELIA: But what really makes them masterpieces — it's how they're all looking at you so intensely. The way their eyes are lit up, it's like they could burn a hole in you. But of course what they were really looking at is *him.* They're staring at him with such joy and such *gratitude,* you can tell it's because in their entire lives nobody ever looked at them the way he's looking at them.

WINSTON: I never, you know, I never thought of it like that.

AMELIA: And you can tell that the way he's looking at them, it's with this

tremendous kind of . . . well, the only word for it is *love*. It's just a
momentary love, and it's certainly a sick and twisted kind of love,
but all the same . . . it's so clear that he loved them.

WINSTON: *(Immediately flaring up.)* Look, don't you have a train to catch?
Can I put you in a cab or something? Because I've got, you know, a
lot of work to do, and frankly this whole conversation is just getting
really annoying. I'm not even sure why you came here.

AMELIA: You know why I'm here. Do you still have it?
*(He pulls out the easel from its resting place and sets it down under the
skylight. He heads into the back room.)*

AMELIA: Walking through those galleries, my heart was pounding so fast,
every time I turned a corner I kept expecting to see my face.
*(He strides back into the front room holding the canvas. He sets it down
on the easel in front of her.)*

WINSTON: Upsettingly enough, this is, I think, the best thing I've ever
done.
*(He steps back toward the wall. She stares at the canvas. Her legs nearly
give way beneath her. She bites her lip to keep from crying. She gets her
water glass from the table and drinks it down in one gulp, her eyes on
the painting. Winston rises and steps toward her.)*

WINSTON: Would you like, um, another glass of water?

AMELIA: Thank you, I would. *(He takes the glass from her and retreats into
the bathroom. Impulsively she goes to the table and picks up the paring
knife. She takes the knife and shoves it toward the canvas as though about
to slash it straight through. Winston comes out of the bathroom.)*

WINSTON: Go ahead. If you want. Please.

AMELIA: *(Turns to him.)* Why bother? It won't make me feel any better.
And at least this way, there's one thing in this world that'll make you
think about me.

WINSTON: *(Aching with regret.)* I am never not thinking about you. *(He
lets out a sob. She stares at him for a moment. Then she puts down the
knife. She gestures toward the canvas.)*

AMELIA: Please: Explain for me what you did here.

WINSTON: It wasn't me. It's all, um, Credeaux. I was just faking it.

AMELIA: Tell me what you were faking, then.

*(He hesitates, then takes a few steps toward the easel. He extends his arms toward the canvas.)*

WINSTON: You proceed as if you're afraid you're about to run out of paint. The end effect being that every gesture is essential, nothing is squandered.

AMELIA: I can see that now.

WINSTON: And with the woman — you try to capture all her contradictory aspects. The way her body is both exposed and concealed, how she's both ashamed and thrilled to be naked.

*(She gazes at the painting with such intensity that it seems as though she might burn a hole in it.)*

WINSTON: And you enhance this in the face: The orange slit of the smile, the flecks of topaz for her eyes — she looks out at you with such fire and such love — you could spend the rest of your life swallowed up in her gaze.

AMELIA: You're right: That's what was there.

WINSTON: But the most important thing is the moon, the way it starts as a tiny peal of light but then it gradually bathes the room, the way it seems like all you have to do is paint the light around her and then you'll discover her inside of it, reaching out for you.

AMELIA: She puts me to shame. *(He stares at her. Her eyes are locked on the canvas.)*

# Degas in New Orleans
Rosary O'Neill

*Dramatic*

Tell (twenties) and Edgar (thirties)

> *In this play, the impressionist painter Edgar Degas visits his brother Rene in New Orleans. Edgar is in love with Rene's wife Tell. In this scene, he confronts her.*
>
> *A two-story rental house on 2306 Esplanade Avenue, New Orleans, Louisiana, 1872. Christmas Eve. Tell Degas, blind and pregnant, enters in a stunning evening gown. She has just said good-bye to her husband and his mistress. She sits among decorations for the cancelled Christmas party. Moments later, Tell's brother-in law Edgar enters. He carefully watches Tell for a few moments and walks slowly to where she sits. She looks tired, miserably sad.*

EDGAR: It's Edgar. Are you all right?

TELL: I'm fine. I'm in alone time. It's necessary, it's difficult, but it's here. See me in the morning, and I'll have a little repartee with you.

EDGAR: *(Moved in spite of himself.)* You're one of the solitaries of the world. *(With fond solicitude.)* We'll celebrate tomorrow.

TELL: *(Bluntly.)* Stop trying to make things right, to understand, to help so much!

EDGAR: Sorry.

TELL: *(Rebukingly.)* You should know better.

EDGAR: It's been a long time since I've had family.

TELL: Start one of your own.

EDGAR: Maybe I should.

TELL: *(With dull anger.)* You've got a ruined Christmas.

EDGAR: I can handle it.

TELL: Will's drunk and not coming with the tree.

EDGAR: That's all right.

TELL: The Christmas party is canceled.

EDGAR: They'll be others.

TELL: *(Cynically brutal.)* Why are you so . . . so complacent?

EDGAR: Because you . . . make me happy.

TELL: I don't know why.

EDGAR: I don't either.

TELL: You annoy me.

> *(She avoids looking in his direction. There is condemnation in her smile mixed with a new violent attraction.)*

EDGAR: *(He tries to copy her coolness but is unable to get over his heartsickness. There is a pause of icy silence. He goes to the window, watches the rain as if he were talking aloud to himself.)* Such a cold moon night. A brittle moon, stone blue. Like your wedding night. The hard darkness of the Cathedral almost gobbles up your bright gown as you come down the aisle. I imagine you are walking to me. I get there an hour before the others just so . . . I can be ready . . . for what I don't know. *(From the window, without turning around.)* Why'd you — marry Rene?

TELL: He made me . . . the right offer.

EDGAR: *(Turning abruptly.)* What is that crap!

TELL: I'd a small child . . . He was willing to live in America.

EDGAR: Off your Papa's money . . . When Rene told me he'd marry you, I accepted it. I adored him, so why shouldn't he have you.

TELL: You were upset?

EDGAR: Crazed . . . Up to the last minute, I thought, prayed you might cancel.

TELL: You never came over.

EDGAR: Why bother? My brother was always there by you. I had to get through him to see you.

TELL: You acted aloof.

EDGAR: *(With a maudlin laugh.)* What in the hell did you expect? The most difficult thing was to say congratulations. Because till I said that you weren't really married.

TELL: You never spoke —

EDGAR: Hearing you say, "I do," I . . . I . . . My body felt like stone. I was cold quiet. But you knew. You knew. It was there all over me, in my eyes, my awkwardness.

TELL: People said you were ill.

EDGAR: *(Wincing his lips, quivering, pitifully.)* I blamed it on a fever yes.

TELL: You left early.

EDGAR: I told myself I'd get through it if I didn't see you. To stay away at all costs. Don't write. Don't —

TELL: We thought you were off painting.

EDGAR: But I was so down, painting became unimportant. *(Shrugs his shoulders — thickly.)* And when I went back to painting, my perspectives were off. I've said about all I can say without —

TELL: *(Protests penitently.)* I thought your role was to paint, that's why I chose Rene. I was a widow tired of crying, hungry for life. *(With sharp irritation.)* You never proposed. I waited . . . and waited.

EDGAR: *(Wrathfully.)* Admit it. You preferred him.

TELL: *(With sudden tenderness.)* Rene was carefree with a childish grandiosity. True. *(Wryly.)* And you sat in the corner with your paintings, quiet, unpredictable, even defiant.

EDGAR: *(Breathes deeply and looks away.)* I couldn't look at you and speak at the same time. And after you left, I kept in motion, traveling about — Rome, London, Madrid — even their visual splendor couldn't keep my eyes from turning inward. Each day I wrote you a letter and each night I tore it up. And no word from you.

TELL: Didn't Didi write?

EDGAR: Yes, but she hardly mentioned you. I combed her letters for clues. Were you happy, sick . . . *(He takes her hand with deep caring.)* I wish I could have been there with you when you lost your sight.

TELL: Me too.

EDGAR: *(His voice grows husky and trembles.)* I would have been your eyes. You could have counted on me.

TELL: *(Half reassured, but frightened.)* How — with you somewhere off . . . Look. I'm married. I can't talk from my heart.

EDGAR: Oh, don't be prim. Not with me. We're two broken souls so . . . let's have one thing complete between us. An honesty "Into Me See."

TELL: *(Clutches her stomach in pain. Startled, Edgar looks about nervously and helps her to the sofa. She looks up at him, pleading frighteningly.)*

All right, I'm going to the end of this . . . or as close to the truth as I can possibly stand.

*(Stricken with a cramp, she stiffens, patting his hand, trying to act normal.)*

EDGAR: Let me call someone.

TELL: No. Now that I've got you here alone, stay with me. Closer. Be with me. Bless me, Father, for I have sinned. For so long I've dreamed of having you here like this, your face by mine. Your hand here.

*(A spasm of pain crosses her face. She squeezes his hand in hers.)*

EDGAR: Let me call Mathilde.

TELL: No. And since you came, I can't sleep. I barely eat and I feel full. I sat before you while you painted, heard the brush on the canvas, smelled the oils, felt your voice all around me and I was totally happy. I wanted to sit there forever, bask in your radiance, feel your eyes on me. That just having you in the same room could make me so delighted. I ordered my fingers to hold on to the chair for fear I'd lift off. You're here leaning over me.

EDGAR: Don't talk.

TELL: *(For the moment she loses all caution.)* I feel like I must have died and gone to heaven. That I could have you beside me to myself. And you could tell me you've been loving me all along. That it's your hand on mine, your eyes looking at me. Your body bending so close. I don't want to move or wake up for fear you'll be gone. I want to live here in this dream.

EDGAR: Let me call your sisters.

TELL: No. . . stay with me. One more moment. *(Another intense cramp.)* OH MY GOD. OH NO. OH MY GOD.

*(Blackout.)*

# Degas in New Orleans
Rosary O'Neill

*Dramatic*

Edgar (thirties) and Rene (twenties)

> *This drama is about a little-known incident in the life of the painter Edgar Degas. In this scene Edgar and his brother Rene discuss the family's dire financial situation.*
>
> *A two-story rental house on 2306 Esplanade Avenue, New Orleans, Louisiana, 1872. Rene Degas moves quickly away from the doorway, feigning concern about an envelope on the desk. Seconds later his brother Edgar comes in, reviewing some bills. He looks at Rene with a quick calculating glance. Walks over to him at the desk. Edgar's hands jerk nervously as he shows Rene a bill. He gives him a strained almost contemptuous glance.*

EDGAR: Tell me if I'm wrong but it doesn't look like you've paid back any of Papa's loans.

RENE: I can't talk about anything else today.

EDGAR: I've got to make some sense out of these records.

RENE: *(Tensely, moves away toward the window.)* As I explained, Papa stopped keeping books for the planters. The old field hands are getting credit from shopkeepers. Railroads and the telegraph are diverting cotton to inland markets and drying up the power base on the river.

EDGAR: Still, we've been selling cotton without exacting a commission?

RENE: *(Ignoring this resentfully.)* I contacted our creditors. I did everything short of sending a drawing with a gun to my temple saying "Pay this or I'll kill myself." I didn't create the financial panic. I've had a short and sorry business life. I don't speak the language, I don't get the nuances of these cotton people. I just want to leave.

*(Abruptly his tone changes to exasperated contrition.)*

If it wasn't for Tell, I'd have left Louisiana. I don't know a single person who wouldn't leave if the means were at hand. The French Quarter is the end of New Orleans, which is the end of Louisiana, which is the end of the world. We're standing at the end of the end.

EDGAR: I'm trying to get some clarity.

RENE: So you can report to Papa what you did right and I've done wrong. *(Rene drinks restlessly, sensing Edgar's struggle to make sense of the invoices.)*

EDGAR: I'm the one who influenced Papa and our sisters and brother to invest in cotton, but you've the control over all his property. That's what Papa wanted, I'm not questioning it.

RENE: Did I run away when Uncle went bankrupt, sold the big house, and moved into this wretched rental property? I'd to get Papa's power of attorney to keep us from starving.

EDGAR: *(Looking down, trying to ignore Rene's tirade.)* But self-dealing will put you in jail.

RENE: True, Papa loaned me too much money. *(Suddenly pointing a finger at Edgar, his voice trembling.)* But he also financed the girls' marriages, your never-ending studies, not to mention the Confederacy. *(Moving a step back, defensively, his face growing hard.)* Papa wanted to turn to you, but trusting me was all he had. Our grandfathers were the geniuses, not him. They made the fortunes in Louisiana cotton and Italian investments. He just inherited their nest egg.

EDGAR: Poor fellow trusted you. You came home raving about Louisiana and telling us all we had to do was give you money for the shears and you'd cut the golden fleece. *(He stares at Rene with increasing enmity, removes a letter.)* Do you know what Papa wrote to me? "I was counting on Rene, who has sent me nothing. Is he going to let our bank, that was held up with so much effort, tumble down? If the creditors put my back against the wall, they'll take me to court." *(Rene crouches on the sofa, picks up his flask listlessly.)*

RENE: Papa's been using the bank to loan himself money. That's why his bank is in trouble.

EDGAR: Fine. Even if I sell a painting a week I can't make enough to stop them from —

RENE: *(He glances away, miserably dogged, drinks.)* American-style business wiped Papa out. I worked hard.

EDGAR: For which you charged us substantial fees. God, we can't have a conversation with you without getting billed. *(Confronting him with the charges.)* Look at this: conversations with Michel Musson, your own uncle, whose house you live in gratis, ten hours. And this, bank deposits for Uncle, conversations with Didi, Mathilde, and Tell Musson. My God, you even billed us for talking to your own wife.
*(Rene shrinks down onto the floor, sitting sideways on an arm of the sofa, so he cannot meet Edgar's eyes.)*

RENE: I charged you a reduced fee.

EDGAR: You knew the cotton business was failing and you gouged funds. You were my favorite brother. God, I trusted you. You had it all, and you took it all.

RENE: *(He jumps up, losing his temper, refusing to admit anything to his brother.)* I am appalled you think I'd do anything unethical. The authorization for my action was Papa's idea. In reference to your . . . accusation . . . about my fees. I and my assistants have spent many hours working . . .

EDGAR: *(Takes a threatening step toward him.)* Such as?

RENE: *(Jeeringly, shoving Edgar back.)* You have benefited . . . directly from the money you have received . . . your gallery openings, your studies, your trips as well as indirectly from Mama and Papa's generosity to you from moneys they've received. It's not my fault the cotton business is failing. I am deeply hurt by your actions as my brother. *(His rage smoldering, he pushes Edgar violently into a chair.)*
If you chastised me for my relationship with America, that I could understand. I feel guilty about that.

EDGAR: *(Edgar's hand goes to his head in an aimless stunned way. He stabilizes himself, looking straight at Rene now. There is a tense pause.)* What is that you are saying? You are sleeping with America? I knew she was helping you with running the house, tending to the children, caring for Tell, but —

RENE: It's been more than that for some time.

EDGAR: You're not . . . You are. You're having relations with her. *(Sharply, letting his resentment come out.)* Here?

RENE: *(With a detached, impersonal tone.)* She understands me. Comforts me.

EDGAR: Your baby is dying, your wife is critically ill, and you're having an affair with her neighbor in her house?

RENE: It didn't start now. It started a year ago.

EDGAR: This is worse than the money. This is Biblical sin. *(Gives a hard, sneering little laugh.)* I can't believe I gave my favorite cousin to you. I let you have her, court her first. And you wasted this possibility. You knew how much I cared. She commanded my attention, and she did so for a long time. *(With threatening anger.)* You couldn't tell me about America all these months I've been here. We all have to deal with unbearable situations. But we don't bring our *mistresses* into our house.

RENE: I hate myself. But God, I'm bored. *(With broken weariness.)* There's no defending it. I've become the men I knew. I wake up and see, like Papa and Uncle, I've a mistress and a wife. *(Rene goes to the window, glad of an excuse to turn his back.)* I want it to end, but it's impossible. I'm too exhausted to break it off. Too disappointed. When we're alone, America's different. She lifts my spirits. *(From the window without turning around.)* No one believes in monogamy anymore. We only choose it when we have no appealing alternatives. Sex is everywhere in a city, except in a husband's relationship with his wife. I say I love my wife, but I'm cold below the neck. I feel nothing. She's attractive to many men, but to me she's not, so I put on a false face. My life is a total lie. Wives dream of other husbands, husbands dream of other wives, and we both shut our eyes.

*(A pause. The brothers avoid looking at each other.)*

EDGAR: Does your wife know about America?

RENE: I guess she suspects. *(Rene comes around in back of his brother, not looking at him, and grabs Edgar's shoulder.)* I don't want to lie, so I'm evasive. It takes so much energy. Believe me, being a liar is tiring. *(Blackout.)*

# Drift
## Jon Tuttle

*Dramatic*

Grady and Louise (thirties)

> *Grady and Louise are a couple in their thirties. This scene takes place in a fast-food joint. Grady is married to someone else, and Louise has finally had enough.*

> *Midday. Louise sits at a bright, plastic-looking table at a burger joint. She wears sunglasses, which she may not take off, and her hand is in a cast or bandage. She's strung out. Nearby are one or two identical tables; Marie sits at one of them, having her lunch and reading a textbook. Presently, Grady enters with a tray of burgers and stuff and sits across from Louise. He gives her a drink with a straw, otherwise, the rest of the food is his.*

GRADY: . . . You OK? This table OK?
  *(Louise shakes her head in disgust.)*
GRADY: . . . OK, I know, look.
LOUISE: What is this.
GRADY: Pepsi.
  *(She pushes it away.)*
GRADY: Look. Just. The thing we gotta do. I've been giving this some thought.
LOUISE: *Have* you.
GRADY: Don't, see, don't —
LOUISE: You've given it —
GRADY: This is exactly what —
LOUISE: You've given it some *thought.* You've given it some thought, and you meet me at, at, at —
GRADY: Don't, don't, don't —
LOUISE: I know why you wanted to come here. What do you think I am?

GRADY: You called *me,* you said *you* —

LOUISE: Do I have "dumbass" stencilled on my forehead?

GRADY: You said *you* wanted —

LOUISE: Do I? Do you see the word "dumbass" on my —

GRADY: No! No! No! . . . OK? . . . Jesus.

*(Pause. Louise gets out a cigarette and lights it.)*

LOUISE: . . . I can't believe this.

GRADY: What'd you do to your hand.

LOUISE: Don't be helpful.

GRADY: I'm asking.

LOUISE: Don't embarrass yourself. *(Pause.)*

GRADY: . . . This is no smoking.

LOUISE: . . . *Oh!*

*(Grady groans.)*

LOUISE: I'm sorry. I thought this was the Dirty Laundry section.

GRADY: Keep your —

LOUISE: *(Loudly.)* I thought this was the Lurid Details section.

GRADY: Sssssshh, sssssshhhh, sssshush! . . . Christ!

*(Pause. Louise smokes. Grady glances over and sees that Marie is looking at them; Marie quickly turns away.)*

LOUISE: . . . You're on it. *(Pause.)* . . . Did you hear me? You're on it.

GRADY: I *know.*

LOUISE: . . . Wanna see it? I showed it to my friend Val. Val says, it's a Latin word, I think it means "shit creek."

GRADY: Who's she.

LOUISE: *He* is a lawyer. *He* is someone I know.

GRADY: You got it?

LOUISE: Do I "got" it? Wanna see it?

GRADY: Lemme see it.

LOUISE: Wanna go over — maybe we could go to Sears and plug it in. We could put it up on the big screen, pull up some lawn chairs.

GRADY: Hey.

LOUISE: You think I'm going to give it to you? You mmm — you boneless —

GRADY: I don't deserve this.

LOUISE: Please.

GRADY: I don't.

LOUISE: You ssss — you squid.

*(Pause. Louise smokes. Marie is chewing, staring straight ahead.)*

GRADY: I thought you said he ignored you . . . He didn't "pay attention" to you.

LOUISE: What I *meant.*

GRADY: Obviously this is not "ignoring" you. Is it.

*(Louise starts to speak, says nothing, shakes her head.)*

GRADY: . . . Who took it.

LOUISE: A guy.

GRADY: What guy.

LOUISE: I don't know, some guy he *paid,* how do I know what *guy?*

GRADY: Where is he, John.

LOUISE: His sister.

GRADY: What does he want.

LOUISE: . . . A *divorce.*

GRADY: . . . He *said* that.

LOUISE: What do you think he *wants.*

GRADY: . . . I think we should remain calm.

LOUISE: . . . I really can't believe this.

GRADY: You talk to him?

LOUISE: I can't.

GRADY: You haven't talked to him.

LOUISE: I *can't* talk to him.

GRADY: You *have* to talk to him. What do you think, you think he's gonna come —

LOUISE: He got a *restraining* order, OK? He got a court *order,* I *can't* talk to him.

*(Pause. Grady sighs — more of a blow, really.)*

LOUISE: . . . She said if I call there again he'll file charges.

GRADY: What'd you *do* to him?

*(Louise has caught Marie looking at them. Marie smiles sheepishly and looks away.)*

GRADY: What'd you *do?*

LOUISE: I can't believe we're sitting h — "I think we have to remain calm."

GRADY: Did you hurt him?

LOUISE: Let's just go.

GRADY: We're getting, let's —

LOUISE: I'm not staying here.

GRADY: We're not, when we, our relationship, when —

LOUISE: Let's go fuck.

GRADY: When we, just listen, just listen for a —

LOUISE: You're my whore. Our "relationship?" *(Pause.)* . . . Aren't you? Say yes. You're my whore.

GRADY: . . . Why are you talking to me this way?

LOUISE: Because you're my whore.

GRADY: Hey.

LOUISE: Whore. Squid.

GRADY: Quit. Calling me that . . .

LOUISE: Do you think I have no dignity? You gelding?

GRADY: You wanna leave? You wanna —

LOUISE: *Yes.* Yes.

GRADY: So go. . . . Go ahead.
   *(Pause. Not what she meant.)*

GRADY: . . . I mean it. Go ahead. *(Pause.)*

LOUISE: . . . You were never any good in bed.

GRADY: So?

LOUISE: . . . *Fuck* you.

GRADY: Fuck *you.* So what?
   *(Pause. Marie is looking at them again.)*

LOUISE: *(To Marie.)* . . . Is this smoke bothering you?
   *(Marie turns away quickly.)*

GRADY: I don't understand why you're doing this.

LOUISE: I have feelings. I have, I —

GRADY: I know you have feelings.

LOUISE: He hurt *me.* Why don't you ask me if —

GRADY: How.

LOUISE: — if he hurt *me,* do you think I am without —

GRADY: What did he do. How did he hurt you.

LOUISE: *(Pleading.)* . . . Can we please . . . just . . . leave? Please?

GRADY: . . . I can't.

LOUISE: Please. Anything. I'm asking. Anything you want, just —

GRADY: I can't, I'm not — I can't.

LOUISE: . . . You can't what.

GRADY: *(Drawing a deep breath.)* . . . I can't. *Be.*

LOUISE: . . . Be what. I don't know that that means, you can't —

GRADY: When we got into this —

LOUISE: — what can't you, what is it you —

GRADY: When we got into this, I'm trying to *tell* you. *(Pause.)* . . . When we got into this . . . OK? We never. . . . Said. . . . We never *said.* That. . . . *We. (Pause.)*

LOUISE: What is this, the fine print?

GRADY: You knew this.

LOUISE: I didn't read the fine print?

GRADY: I have a *wife.* . . . You knew this. . . . You *knew* this.

LOUISE: . . . Well *you* knew that. Didn't you know that?

GRADY: What are you asking me.

LOUISE: You *hate* your wife.

GRADY: Think about what you're asking me.

LOUISE: She hates *you,* this is a quote, isn't it? She hates you, she doesn't "want" you anymore, she "turns her back" on you. This is something you *said. (Pause.)* . . . Do you think you can just walk away? . . . *Now?* You can just.

GRADY: I have a family.

LOUISE: Why are you doing this?

*(He doesn't answer. Long pause.)*

LOUISE: . . . I gave up my marriage for you.

GRADY: No, actually, you did not.

LOUISE: Obviously yes, I did.

GRADY: No, I was, I was . . . "incidental." To it. . . . I was an accessory.

LOUISE: . . . You *have* been giving this some thought.

GRADY: I was extraneous. . . . Or yes: I was your whore. Yes.

LOUISE: . . . Mmm. Mmm. . . . And what was I?

GRADY: What were you?

LOUISE: Yes. *(Pause.)*

GRADY: *(As diplomatically as possible.)* . . . You. Were the one. You were the one. . . . who got caught. First.

*(Pause. She looks at him — hard. Tableau lights to black.)*

# Exposition Boulevard
Rosary O'Neill


*Dramatic*

Susanne and Blaise (twenties)

> *This play takes place in a mansion in New Orleans. Susanne is a celebrity painter; Blaise is an actor. Susanne is in love with Blaise, who is unhappily married.*

> *The gallery and front parlor of a mansion on Exposition Boulevard, New Orleans. Early evening. The present. Susanne appears dressed in an exotic gown. Finding herself alone, she moves to the liquor cabinet, downs some vodka, fills the bottle with water.*

SUSANNE: "Soft you now! The fair Ophelia. — Nymph, in thy orisons. Be all thy sins rememb'red." Oh . . . he's scribbled my name in the margin. What does it say? Can't make it out. There's a bleeding heart. Mn. This calls for music.
*(She moves to the stereo, turns it on, dances sensually around the gallery. Blaise, an actor, enters. He is handsome, late twenties, tall, long limbed with a wide forehead, thick brown hair, and fine sensitive eyes. He wears conservative dark evening attire, obviously expensive, and he wears it well. He pauses in the doorway, his eyes darting up and down her body.)*
BLAISE: You're early? My wife's not home.
SUSANNE: *(She smiles.)* I love rain on an unexpected day. Every pore opens to the wind.
BLAISE: Shouldn't you be getting ready?
*(He wipes his face with a handkerchief, swallows water. She strolls over and . . . )*
SUSANNE: How are you newlyweds making out?
BLAISE: *(Retrieves his glass, walks on the veranda.)* Fine. Most of the guys

I grew up with are still here. Sundays you'll see them running baby carriages through the park. Weekdays the wives race walk and —

SUSANNE: Recount their husband's infidelities? You still have soft feelings for me?

BLAISE: *(With a flickering smile.)* Don't. The love disease is fatal and progressive. My therapy is not to pursue a sexy woman one day at a time, and to hang out with other recovering husbands and not talk about it. *(She turns up the music, resumes dancing a step. He watches her, his eyes moist.)*

SUSANNE: Your hair's fallen over your face. I'll get it.

BLAISE: Stop. I hasten to tell you. Moses came down from the mountain and said. "I come bearing good news and bad news. The good news is I got him down to ten. The bad news is adultery is still in."

SUSANNE: That's in the Far East. If you accept a provincial marriage in the South, it's a sort of burial. *(Dance music swells from the stereo.)* Dance with me.

BLAISE: Why?

SUSANNE: The assumption we'll start with is we're not finished.

BLAISE: Is that right?

SUSANNE: Not a lot of activity now that we've heard the crickets and had a little talk.

BLAISE: Don't touch.

SUSANNE: Before you, I knew a kiss was something you did with your mouth, but I didn't know what it was.

BLAISE: My wife will be here.

SUSANNE: Let me enjoy you — arms length at a safe distance. Don't stop dancing till the lights go out.

*(She lifts his arms, stretches them around her, draws his head near hers. She cradles his face. He freezes momentarily like a deer sensing hunters.)*

BLAISE: You and I after all. *(Drawing away.)* Shame upon you, Susanne.

SUSANNE: Don't walk away. If you're going to say something, say it to my face.

BLAISE: The best way to remember something is to put it behind you.

SUSANNE: You're teasing me.

BLAISE: You know me better.

SUSANNE: I know how you squeezed me in the dark whenever I came near.

I saw you when you walked down the aisle. You loved me then and you do now.

BLAISE: That's a strange thing to say —

SUSANNE: I've dreamt of you since I saw you. I've a sixth sense, and my thoughts have flown to you.

BLAISE: Don't.

SUSANNE: I can't wait for dreaming. And now you say to tear your memory for my eyes? I won't. I can't.

*(The veranda lights blink on. Suddenly Susanne is all nerves and sobs. She buries her head in his shoulder.)*

BLAISE: Ssh. Let's go inside.

SUSANNE: Why didn't you shoot me, as you threatened? I wish you'd shoot me now —

BLAISE: I hate myself for . . . You took the last of the food money and used it for liquor. I was crazy with worry, and when I found you with the guy next door.

SUSANNE: He was nothing.

BLAISE: It wasn't a question of my love for you. The dog-eat-dog lifestyle tore us apart. If we could come up with a pack of cigarettes between the two of us, it was shocking.

SUSANNE: How could you run off to New York?

BLAISE: I told you what happened in L.A. I got that soap opera in New York. I thought I'd make a bundle. Selling chunks of my soul at varying intervals. A month later I went on unemployment. My ego was so battered. I had to have . . . What could I promise you but a life of poverty? My wife . . . well —

SUSANNE: You should have called.

BLAISE: Lucille really cares for me.

SUSANNE: You should have written.

BLAISE: Calm down.

SUSANNE: I don't care who hears. I've been having anxiety attacks. I'm scared all the time and feel alone. I need you to be there to believe in me. I'm tired of a life of not having you.

# Flaming Guns of the Purple Sage

Jane Martin

*Comic*

Shedevil and Rob (twenties)

> *Shedevil is a colorfully dressed, weird biker-chick, hiding out from a crazed biker who wants to kill her. Rob is a rodeo cowboy on the mend from an injury whose entire reality is western B movies.*

> *Rob appears on the stairs with a silver-plated traditional cowboy six-shooter in his hand. He wears only a jockstrap.*

ROB: Turn around real slow. I got you covered.
   *(She turns. She laughs.)*
ROB: Excuse me, I was sleepin'.
   *(She continues to laugh.)*
ROB: It's the way God made us, OK?
SHEDEVIL: OK, nutcase, now what?
ROB: Damn, you look pretty. Whew. Lookin' like ice water on a hot day. Darn. I get this. I get what this is. Sure, I recognize it. Oh, man, I seen this in *Bells of Rosarita, Plainsman and the Lady.* By golly, straight out of *Cimarron Petticoats.*
SHEDEVIL: What the hell are you talking about?
ROB: Love at first sight.
SHEDEVIL: Kaboom, whack.
ROB: It happens between the hero and the schoolmarm, or sometimes it's the deceased kindly rancher's daughter an' the travelin' sheriff, has amnesia from the avalanche. *(He's still holding the gun on her.)* Put the bags down, OK?
   *(She does.)*

ROB: Never thought it would come on me 'cause I ain't the hero, I'm sort of more the young man the hero befriends. See? 'Cept they usually got their clothes on.

SHEDEVIL: Hey, doofus, I got to find Lucifer Lee and, yo, I can't do it on twenty dollars.

ROB: Love at first sight. Boy, it's painful.

SHEDEVIL: What good's a bunch of silver buckles in a shoebox?

ROB: 'At's all the cowboys Big Eight has healed.

SHEDEVIL: Yeah?

ROB: What's love at first sight feel like to you?

SHEDEVIL: You're retarded, huh?

ROB: Beg your pardon?

*(Sound of a motorcycle.)*

SHEDEVIL: *(Holds out her hand for silence.)* Motorcycle. *(Rob Bob opens front door.)* No! *(They listen; it approaches; it roars by.)* Wasn't him.

ROB: How'd ya know!

SHEDEVIL: It's some two-bit Japanese bike. OK, here's the deal. I'll go upstairs with you. Then I leave with the buckles.

ROB: Lord, I 'preciate that, but I'm savin' myself for marriage.

SHEDEVIL: What about Big whatsername?

ROB: Well, that don't count. That's customary.

SHEDEVIL: She screwed every one of these buckles?

ROB: Just a mark a' respect. Like when Gene or Roy tip their hat to the saloon lady when they ride off.

SHEDEVIL: Shazaam!

ROB: Beggin' your pardon, but what's them noises?

SHEDEVIL: Nuthin'.

ROB: Hey, they're somethin'.

SHEDEVIL: Just started when my daddy'd lock me in the basement.

ROB: My daddy locked me in the basement too!

SHEDEVIL: No way.

ROB: Yeah! Well, we didn't have a basement, kinda chained me under the house.

SHEDEVIL: Yeah? How come you sleep in a jockstrap?

ROB: I don't like woolly pajamas. Say, I got mucho respect you're huntin' for your husband.

SHEDEVIL: Whatever.

ROB: Sounds like he's bad though.

SHEDEVIL: Like in those movies?

ROB: Yeah. See, there's good people an' bad people, an' funny sidekicks an' the love interests, an' the bystanders, which it don't matter what they are.

SHEDEVIL: *(Sort of charmed.)* Yeah?

ROB: Yeah. Now, the good people, no matter what happens, what they have to do . . . whatever . . . they are good people, an' the bad people, they're bad.

SHEDEVIL: So what am I in the movie?

ROB: Schoolmarm.

SHEDEVIL: I look like a schoolmarm?

ROB: You look real nice in that white dress.

SHEDEVIL: What about me takin' the buckles?

ROB: It's real sweet 'cause you're doin' it fer your unborn child. Now, if you were one of the bad people, it would be bad to do it.

SHEDEVIL: You're goofy as hell, huh?

ROB: I guess.

SHEDEVIL: Listen, can I ask you a question?

ROB: Yes, ma'am.

SHEDEVIL: Does it bother you talkin' to me bare ass?

ROB: Guess I mainly forgot about it. *(Looks down at himself.)* Didn't mean no harm.

SHEDEVIL: It's OK. *(A pause: They look at each other.)* Cowboy, what the hell are you going to do now?

ROB: Well, in a love-at-first-sight deal, we could do a little kiss. Nothin' real involved.

SHEDEVIL: I don't have the love-at-first-sight deal.

ROB: Shore you do. 'Member back now. I came round the corner. Our eyes met like. It was real still.

SHEDEVIL: You scared me pissless.

ROB: It feels like that.

SHEDEVIL: You were pointing the gun!

ROB: That jes' gives the love scene a little pep. Little originality. It's still a damn love scene. Looky here . . . you go to the movie an' there's a boy an' a girl . . . you followin' me?

SHEDEVIL: You know, you're talking when we could be screwing.

ROB: Ummm, no, I didn't know that.

SHEDEVIL: You nervous or what?

ROB: Well, sort of am, yeah.

SHEDEVIL: OK, kiss me then.

ROB: You don't mind I'm in the buff?

SHEDEVIL: I can deal with it.

ROB: I'm jus' gonna kiss the outside of your lips now.

SHEDEVIL: OK.

ROB: Real easy like.

SHEDEVIL: OK.

ROB: Tilt your head up.

SHEDEVIL: Shut up, OK?

ROB: OK. *(He moves toward her, putting the six-shooter on the butcher block as he comes. He stops a step from her.)* Close your eyes.

SHEDEVIL: I don't close my eyes.

ROB: You sure?

SHEDEVIL: I'm sure.

ROB: Well, people got to get used to each other.

SHEDEVIL: Smack!

*(She puts her arms around his neck.)*

ROB: Smack right back atcha.

*(They kiss gently. The lights fade.)*

# The Hologram Theory
Jessica Goldberg

*Dramatic*

Patsy and Dominic (twenties)

> *In this scene Patsy, a beautiful young Trinidadian artist, awakens one night to a vision of her brother Dominic, whom she hasn't seen in five years. Turns out, he has been murdered, and his ghost has come to ask her to solve the mystery of his death and his life.*

> *A bed in a bedroom in Trinidad. Patsy sleeps, the room is shadowy, airy. Dominic appears in a shadow, barely seen.*

DOMINIC: Patsy. Pat. Patsy. *(Patsy moves in the bed.)* Pssst. Patsy, oh gosh girl I got to tell you something. Patsy. Yoo hoo.
  *(Patsy sits up, startled.)*
PATSY: Dominic?
DOMINIC: Yeah, Patsy?
PATSY: That you?
DOMINIC: Yes.
PATSY: My God, you come home.
DOMINIC: Yes, sister.
  *(Patsy sits up, excited.)*
PATSY: You scared me. Come, come into the light, let me see you. Mama's gonna be so excited. Sometimes she say she don't think she ever gonna see you again.
DOMINIC: You alone?
PATSY: Who I be with? You moved five years ago.
DOMINIC: You still go with Bertram?
PATSY: Yeah. Come, I don't believe you're really here —
DOMINIC: So where is he? You guys have a fight or something?
PATSY: No. He won't sneak in anymore, says I have to marry him. Don't

worry, happens all the time, every three days or so. He'll be back soon. Bertram has no discipline.

DOMINIC: Or you be so sexy he can't resist.

PATSY: C'mon, c'mhere, let me hug you.

DOMINIC: Anyways Bertram's right. You should be gettin' married, you is twenty-seven now, is what you waitin' for?

PATSY: Still want to go to college.

DOMINIC: Please, you gonna be eighty lyin' in bed in your mother's house, waitin' to go to college, hopin' your man got tired of jerkin' off.

PATSY: Ah ah hold on, brother. I'm gettin' to be a good painter, soon they be acceptin' me at all the best schools. Full tuition.

DOMINIC: Soon as you apply.

PATSY: Ya see still the same ol' smart mouth. Before I kick you outta here, come let me see you.

*(Dominic moves into the light. He wears simple khaki pants and a light shirt. His feet are bare.)*

PATSY: God bless mih eyesight!

*(Dominic smiles.)*

PATSY: Like ya never left!

DOMINIC: Same person.

PATSY: Yah, you lookin' like the spittin' image of the day ya left, except then ya had on shoes then.

DOMINIC: Couldn't resist the feelin' of my country 'gainst me feet.

PATSY: I don't know what I was expectin'.

DOMINIC: Disappointed?

PATSY: No, in fact it makes me happy ta see ya this way after five years.

DOMINIC: We don't like change, do we much? Us Trinis.

PATSY: Sometimes I'se be starin' at the tourists on the beach, some of 'em black, ya know, and I'm thinkin', that Dominic? that Dominic? And I get this fear that you changed and you don't want me to recognize ya.

DOMINIC: We're twins, Patsy. I'se be your other half, you in me, me in you, Orisha Marassa, 'course you always gonna recognize me.

PATSY: Orisha Marassa . . . boy, haven't heard that in a long time.

DOMINIC: I write to ya tellin' you how I been worshippin' the Orisha.

PATSY: Yeah, but what about that, eh? Ya never step foot inside a temple when ya live here. Granny was all the time beggin' us to come, come, I went, you say that's old-school stupidness.

DOMINIC: One day, Patsy, away from home, tryin' hard ta be someone, things change. Need to get back to your roots.

PATSY: Makes me happy to hear, I was afraid when ya left ya wasn't never gonna look back. Now you're here, so come hug me, brother!

DOMINIC: Can't hug ya, Patsy.

PATSY: Why not?

DOMINIC: Not really here.

PATSY: How ya mean? I be dreamin'?

DOMINIC: I dead. No body ta hold anymore, see, touch for yourself — *(Dominic reaches his hand out to her. She goes to touch it. There is nothing there. She's shocked.)* — No body anymore —

PATSY: — Nothin' there —

DOMINIC: — Dead, Patsy.

# The Hologram Theory
Jessica Goldberg

*Dramatic*

Julian and Mimi (twenties)

>*Julian wants to have sex with Mimi. She's past all that.*

JULIAN: *(Quietly.)* Mi. Mimi. Mi.
>*(She jumps, startled, stares forward.)*
MIMI: What?
JULIAN: Do you believe in God?
MIMI: What?
JULIAN: God.
MIMI: I don't know, Julian.
JULIAN: Yeah.
>*(She is quiet, still staring out.)*
JULIAN: I want to pray.
MIMI: I'm sleeping.
JULIAN: Tell me how?
MIMI: What?
JULIAN: Tell me how to pray.
MIMI: I don't know.
JULIAN: Shit.
MIMI: Are you dreaming?
JULIAN: Nightmares, only I'm awake.
MIMI: C'mon.
JULIAN: Do you love me?
MIMI: What?
>*(Julian clasps his hands in prayer on her bed.)*
JULIAN: Please God —
MIMI: I'm gonna go away, Julian —
JULIAN: Make it stop, the nightmare —

MIMI: It's the smell, it's stinking up the place, but I'm afraid to move it.
Thank God I'm out of here, something's wrong with my circulation.
My body parts keep falling asleep.

JULIAN: I love Mimi, God?

MIMI: You scare me, stop. *(She pushes him on the floor. He lies there, quiet.)*

JULIAN: Do you have to go away?

MIMI: Yes.

JULIAN: When?

MIMI: My last final is Friday, then I'm off to Europe.

JULIAN: You hate me.

MIMI: Shut up.

JULIAN: I wanted to put on a shirt, but he was in the closet —

MIMI: Shut up.

JULIAN: You're so pretty, Mimi.

MIMI: You're so . . . annoying.

JULIAN: C'I come in the bed with you?

MIMI: No.

JULIAN: C'I sleep on the floor?

MIMI: No.

JULIAN: I'll have sex with you.

MIMI: I don't want to have sex with you.

JULIAN: Why not?

MIMI: I'm over it.

JULIAN: Pleeeze, Mimi?

MIMI: What?

JULIAN: Lemme come in the bed.

MIMI: Fine.

*(Julian comes in the bed.)*

JULIAN: He was in the closet, just his head looking at me, you know —
'cause that night, Mi? Do you know anyone that knows how to pray?

MIMI: Uhmmmm . . .

JULIAN: I think that's what I should do.

MIMI: There's Jews for Jesus on campus.

JULIAN: That's a good idea. You're so smart, Mimi. Will you rub my head?

MIMI: C'mon.

JULIAN: You're leaving me anyway.

MIMI: You're gonna live with my stepsister.

JULIAN: Is she like you?

MIMI: No.

JULIAN: What's she like?

MIMI: Uhmmm . . .

JULIAN: Does she pray?

MIMI: No way. *(Quiet, Mimi rubs Julian's head.)*

JULIAN: Mimi, are you asleep?

MIMI: No.

JULIAN: What are you doing?

MIMI: Thinking.

JULIAN: About God?

MIMI: My stepsister.

JULIAN: See, I think God's my only hope —

MIMI: I don't really know her. I love her, I guess. I wish she loved me, then we could be real sisters, you know? My mother and her father moved to Paris, should I visit them? When I backpack?

JULIAN: I want it to go away, Mimi —

MIMI: It would be fun to have a sister, or a brother . . .

JULIAN: I want to sleep, you know?

MIMI: Yeah. Buck will protect us.

JULIAN: Buck will protect us.

MIMI: Will he?

JULIAN: Yes. You're so cozy.

MIMI: Thanks.

JULIAN: I love you.

MIMI: Yeah.

JULIAN: I can sleep with you 'cause I love you, and if I loved God, then maybe I could sleep alone —

MIMI: Shhh . . . Shhh . . . go to sleep. Go to sleep.

# The Hologram Theory
Jessica Goldberg

*Dramatic*

Sarah (twenties to thirties) and Simon (forties)

> *This scene takes place in a New York City bar. Simon is a famous writer. Sara is interviewing him.*
>
> *A bar on the Upper East Side. Simon enters the restaurant where Sara waits. Simon is well dressed, cool. Sara stands. Simon comes to the table.*

SIMON: Sarah Lipmann.

SARAH: Is it obvious?

SIMON: Most things are apparent. *(They shake, sit.)*

SARAH: It is an honor and a pleasure to meet you.

SIMON: Warming up your meat.

SARAH: No, I'm sincere. I'm a huge fan of your work. I took the liberty of ordering us a bottle of wine. Can I pour you a drink?

SIMON: Please.

> *(Sara pours.)*

SIMON: Do you know what one of my favorite things about being famous is?

SARAH: Tell me.

SIMON: A woman who wouldn't give you the time of day, half your age, sits across from you, her eyes gleaming, prepared to listen to any stupid thing that comes out of your mouth.

SARAH: Cheers.

> *(They clink glasses.)*

SARAH: I'm sure any woman would listen to anything you had to say whether or not you were famous. You're a very handsome man.

SIMON: You're very good.

SARAH: It's my job. *(They drink.)* Your story has been very inspiring to me.

SIMON: I came to New York City with five dollars in my pocket and my mother in tow. It wasn't easy, but every time I was about to give up I dreamt of returning to my home town — Huntsville — hearing whispers, my name — they'd be sorry. My father, the cheerleaders who wouldn't fuck me, teachers, the colleges who refused me scholarships. I fought to be someone. It pains me that my children will never have the experience I had.

SARAH: My stepsister and I are about ten years apart — we grew up so differently. Tell me about your children.

SIMON: I have three lovely children. I plan to make sure that they understand work.

SARAH: I thought four?

SIMON: Four?

SARAH: Four children.

SIMON: A child with my first wife, yes.

SARAH: Julian.

SIMON: How do you know?

SARAH: I do my research.

SIMON: And what does your research tell you about my son Julian?

SARAH: Just his name.

SIMON: Yes, Julian is a product of an ideal bourgeois marriage.

SARAH: Meaning?

SIMON: My new wife and I have a very unconventional marriage, and yet have managed to have three lovely productive children.

SARAH: But they're young.

SIMON: Meaning?

SARAH: You can't exactly be sure if they'll be productive yet.
    *(Simon laughs.)*

SIMON: You have a lot of opinions for an interviewer.

SARAH: Do I?

SIMON: I like that in a woman. And an interview.

SARAH: What do you mean by an "unconventional" marriage?

SIMON: Whatever you'd like it to mean, dear.
    *(Sarah laughs.)*

SIMON: And you?

SARAH: Me?

SIMON: Do you have children?

SARAH: Oh no.

SIMON: Married?

SARAH: No.

SIMON: In a relationship?

SARAH: Never.

SIMON: What do you do for pleasure?

SARAH: Interview.

SIMON: And sex?

SARAH: I believe I'm the one conducting this interview.

SIMON: You work too hard, Sarah.

SARAH: I love my work.

SIMON: Work is within our control.

SARAH: I like control.

SIMON: I was enamored of my son Julian, struck by the miracle of this creature I produced. The first one is like that, a piece of you. The sensation fades with the fourth. I thought, this is my greatest creation. Now I will truly be able to see that part of myself that appears to me only in my work. But that's not the way it is, he may as well have been adopted. I'm telling you something very personal you understand.

SARAH: I saw a photo of him. There's a lot of resemblance.

SIMON: Oh he is certainly mine.

SARAH: More than you think. You're both very beautiful. Your beauty is hard. His is soft still. I think he is definitely a part of you.

SIMON: You're a strange woman.

SARAH: I don't quite know how to take that "strange."

SIMON: It's a compliment. Coming from me. Cheers.

# Human Events

## A. R. Gurney

*Seriocomic*

Anita and Porter  (forties)

> *Anita and Porter are both college professors. Both have a problem with an adjunct professor who is basically taking over their department. In this scene, Anita asks Porter over to discuss the problem, but it becomes clear she has something else in mind entirely.*

> *Anita comes on, carrying a tray with a bottle and two glasses.*

ANITA: How about some sherry, Porter? Chris gave me a bottle for my birthday.

PORTER: *(Joining her.)* Thanks.

*(They settle on the pillows.)*

ANITA: *(Pouring.)* I don't normally hold meetings in my apartment, Porter. But unlike my male counterparts, I have to be home when my children get out of school.

PORTER: Nice place.

ANITA: Tiny. *(Indicating off.)* The bedroom is nothing but bed. *(Sipping sherry.)* Now. What gives? I found your rather cryptic request on my desk.

PORTER: I'd like to teach a section of your writing course, Anita.

ANITA: You? Stuffy old Porter Platt? Teaching writing?

PORTER: As you may have heard, I'm having trouble getting into my book. Maybe I need a few stretch exercises.

ANITA: Don't we all.

PORTER: The Dean said your course had too many students.

ANITA: I do! It's a gas! They're clambering to get in, now that it fulfills a basic Humanities credit. We can all thank Chris for that.

PORTER: I don't thank Chris for anything.

ANITA: You were such close friends.

PORTER: I can't teach under him. Leave it at that.

ANITA: But isn't this rather ridiculous? Me, a lowly lecturer, interviewing a tenured professor for a funky little course in creative writing. Why not just go ahead and teach it?

PORTER: Because the Dean says it's your course and you have the right to decide.

ANITA: Then I'd like to see a specimen.

PORTER: Of my urine?

ANITA: Of your writing, silly. I ask it of everyone involved. Including myself.

PORTER: My last article was published two years ago in *The Sewanee Review*. You can get it in the library.

ANITA: Oh Porter. I'm not interested in your scholarly work. The title of this course is "Writing and the Self," remember? We will be searching for our own personal voice. Now here . . . *(She gets a pad and ballpoint pen.)* Write something. A paragraph, a sentence, maybe even just a phrase — which feels real and honest and true.

PORTER: Here? Now?

ANITA: Why not?

*(Porter takes the pen, starts to write, then stops.)*

PORTER: I can't. I feel too much under the gun.

ANITA: Don't be silly.

PORTER: *(Tries again; stops.)* Nope. Still can't. As Byron says, "The caged eagle cannot mate."

*(Pause.)*

ANITA: You feel caged, Porter?

PORTER: Maybe tonight when I get home . . .

ANITA: You still won't be able to do it.

PORTER: Why do you say that?

ANITA: Because you're hung up, Porter Platt.

PORTER: Hung up?

ANITA: On something you don't dare deal with.

PORTER: And what might that be?

ANITA: Christopher Simpson.

    *(Pause.)*

PORTER: Go on.

ANITA: Do you want me to spell it out?

PORTER: Please do.

ANITA: I find this somewhat embarrassing.

PORTER: Are you by any chance saying . . . ?

ANITA: I think I am.

PORTER: Oh Anita, for shit's sake! You're always running around saying
    everybody's gay.

ANITA: Lately it seems that everybody is.

PORTER: Well I'm not, thanks.

ANITA: You are certainly obsessed with the man.

PORTER: I'm pissed off at the man.

ANITA: You bent over backwards to get him in here.

PORTER: I'd bend over forwards to get him out.

ANITA: See? Gay.

PORTER: Oh shit.

ANITA: There's nothing wrong with being gay, Porter.

PORTER: Except that I'm not.

ANITA: *(A big sip of sherry.)* Prove it.

PORTER: How do I prove a negative?

ANITA: By being positive.

PORTER: *(Getting up.)* I'm outa here.

ANITA: *(Standing in his way.)* You're walking away from it.

PORTER: Move, Anita!

ANITA: How can I possibly let you teach the Self when you're so out of
    touch with your own?

PORTER: *(Trying to push past her.)* Let me pass, please, Anita.

ANITA: You've "passed" all your life, haven't you? Isn't it time to release?

PORTER: *(Grabbing her shoulders.)* Release? Release? How? By kissing the
    guy? Like this? *(He kisses her angrily.)*

ANITA: That was a very cold kiss, Porter.

PORTER: Oh it's warmth you want. How about this? *(Kisses her again.)*

ANITA: Now you're angry.

PORTER: I've got to get back.

ANITA: I can't let you leave like this. *(Taking out a handkerchief.)* At least let me wipe your fevered brow . . . *(She does; she wipes the inside of his collar.)* You are hot under the collar, aren't you?

PORTER: How'd you guess?

ANITA: Do you think anger is an aphrodisiac, Porter?

PORTER: Maybe.

ANITA: I do. I think that's why the Greeks had the god of war conjoin with the goddess of love . . . *(Putting her handkerchief away.)* Now go, if you want.

PORTER: Give me another sherry, Anita . . .

ANITA: Say please.

PORTER: *(Takes her glass; downs it.)* Now I want to see the rest of your apartment. *(Takes her toward the bedroom.)*

ANITA: The bed isn't even made.

PORTER: *(Pulling her.)* So much the better.

ANITA: Hey! I thought the caged eagle couldn't mate.

PORTER: Fuck the caged eagle.

*(He pulls her offstage. Blackout. Erotic music. Lights up. Porter comes on, buttoning his shirt.)*

PORTER: There.

*(Anita comes on, buttoning her blouse.)*

ANITA: Whatever that means.

PORTER: How was that for self-expression, baby?

ANITA: I'd say it was fraught with ambiguity.

PORTER: Oh yes?

ANITA: Some people might even call it a rape.

PORTER: Oh yeah? Who raped whom, I'd like to know.

ANITA: I'll say this: If I weren't committed to pass/fail, I'd give it a C minus.

PORTER: At least I proved something.

ANITA: Whatever you proved, Porter, I won't take it to the Women's Grievance Committee if you don't bandy it about in the halls.

PORTER: It's a deal. *(He starts out.)*

ANITA: Wait, Porter. One thing.

*(He stops.)*

ANITA: Please don't teach in my course. You'll just screw up your students, you're such a mess.

PORTER: So are you, Anita.

ANITA: I know I am. But at least I admit it.

*(A buzzer sounds.)*

ANITA: There are my kids. Scoot, lover. Out the back.

# In Arabia
# We'd All Be Kings
Stephen Adly Guirgis

*Dramatic*

Charlie and Chickie (twenties)

> *Chickie is a crackhead hooker and Charlie's a rather simple-minded bartender who thinks he's a Jedi warrior and kind of looks out for Chickie, buying her meals in hopes that they maybe could go out sometime.*

> *Monday, late morning. The bar.*

CHARLIE: Have you got a eight?

CHICKIE: No.

CHARLIE: You're supposed to say "Go Fish."

CHICKIE: Oh.

CHARLIE: Have you got a nine?

CHICKIE: No.

CHARLIE: Chickie?!

CHICKIE: What?

CHARLIE: You gotta say, "Go Fish."

CHICKIE: Oh.

CHARLIE: So say it then.

CHICKIE: Go Fish.

CHARLIE: Your turn.

CHICKIE: OK, um, do you have a nine?

CHARLIE: Yeah.

CHICKIE: I'll take that, thank you very much.

CHARLIE: Wait a sec, Chickie. I just axed you do you gotta nine and you said no, so how come now you gotta nine!

CHICKIE: I don't know.

CHARLIE: You do too know!

CHICKIE: No I don't.

CHARLIE: If I ax you do you got something and you got it, you gotta give it to me.

CHICKIE: Why?

CHARLIE: 'Cuz, that's the game, understand?

CHICKIE: Yeah.

CHARLIE: OK . . . You gotta Jack?

CHICKIE: No.

CHARLIE: C'mon Chickie, I know you gotta Jack.

CHICKIE: No.

CHARLIE: Chickie, look me in my eye and tell me you ain't got no Jack?

CHICKIE: . . . Oh, OK, here.

CHARLIE: Thank you.

CHICKIE: You happy?

CHARLIE: Yeah, I'm very happy.

CHICKIE: You don't look happy.

CHARLIE: . . . It's your turn.

CHICKIE: I don't wanna play. I'm hungry.

CHARLIE: You wanna eat something?

CHICKIE: Yeah.

CHARLIE: Whaddya wanna eat?

CHICKIE: Fish! Shrimps!

CHARLIE: You can't eat shrimps for breakfast. Shrimps are for lunch or dinner, not breakfast.

CHICKIE: Can I eat lunch or dinner with you?

CHARLIE: If you want.

CHICKIE: OK.

CHARLIE: Breakfast is for Egg McMuffins and chocolate milk, maybe some cereals, or, like, if it's Sunday or a special day, you could have pancakes and bacon or waffles wit' whip cream, somethin' like that. Oh! You know what?

CHICKIE: What?

CHARLIE: You could have salmon for breakfast, that's a breakfast thing.

CHICKIE: What's salmon?

CHARLIE: Whaddya mean?

CHICKIE: I mean, what's salmon?

CHARLIE: You don't know what a salmon is?

CHICKIE: What is it?

CHARLIE: A salmon is a salmon. It's a pink fish.

CHICKIE: Is it good?

CHARLIE: I don't know, but it's a fish.

CHICKIE: How about pizza?

CHARLIE: A pizza's not a fish, Chickie.

CHICKIE: Duh!! I know that! I mean, How 'bout pizza? For breakfast?

CHARLIE: Pizza for breakfast?

CHICKIE: Yeah . . . Pleeeease???

CHARLIE: OK, pizza it is.

CHICKIE: From the Arab place, OK?

CHARLIE: The Arabs?!

CHICKIE: Please??

CHARLIE: OK, from the Arabs.

CHICKIE: Sometimes I think you're nicer than my boyfriend.

CHARLIE: I am nicer than your boyfriend.

CHICKIE: No you're not. *(Pause.)*

CHARLIE: I gotta go wash some glasses. Here's some dough for the pizza.

CHICKIE: You gotta girlfriend, Charlie?

CHARLIE: . . . Yeah. I got five girlfriends.

CHICKIE: How come they never come around?

CHARLIE: 'Cuz they don't live here.

CHICKIE: Charlie? Do you think some time we could do something? I mean, not as girlfriend and boyfriend, but, like, the way we are now?

CHARLIE: Yeah, we could do that.

CHICKIE: Charlie?

CHARLIE: Yeah?

CHICKIE: How come you're so big but Jose kicked your ass, and Jimmy and RaRa, they kicked your ass too?

CHARLIE: I don't know.

CHICKIE: And that guy Ronnie, and that crazy guy with the hat that time, they kicked your ass too. Even my boyfriend could prolly kick your ass.

CHARLIE: I don't think so.

CHICKIE: Everybody always kicks his ass too, but he's little. My boyfriend, he always says, "If I was big as that retard" —

CHARLIE: — What retard?

CHICKIE: Not you! Someone else!

CHARLIE: Who?

CHICKIE: I don't know.

CHARLIE: Lemme tell you something, Chickie . . . You ever watch the *Star Wars* movies?

CHICKIE: Yeah.

CHARLIE: You know what a Jedi fighter is?

CHICKIE: No.

CHARLIE: Chickie, a Jedi fighter is Hans Solo and Obi Wan Kenobi and those guys over there. Even Darth Vader, you know Darth Vader?

CHICKIE: Yes.

CHARLIE: Even he was a Jedi fighter, but he used his powers for bad, so now he gotta wear a mask and shit. Jedi fighters get powers, like, they could do anything, OK?

CHICKIE: Yeah.

CHARLIE: Ya understand?

CHICKIE: Yeah.

CHARLIE: OK. I'm gonna tell you something, Chickie . . . Me, I'm a Jedi fighter.

CHICKIE: Charlie?

CHARLIE: I'm serious, I got a Jedi name and everything. And I got powers. A lot of powers, but I can't use them for bad, or else, I gotta wear a mask like Darth Vader, and I don't think that would fly too good in the city. I got special powers, but, why am I gonna waste them on Jimmy and Jose and RaRa and those guys? I can't take the risk to lose my powers by accidentally doing bad against them. But lemme tell you this: If me and you was to go out "just as friends" and somebody tried to mess wit' you or do you harm, you better believe I would use all my Jedi powers against them, even if I had to cross the line against them and do bad to them, even if I had to wear a mask for the rest a my life because a it. I wouldn't care, 'cuz you would be protected and safe, and even if they took me to jail, I would give you money first so you could go eat shrimps, OK?

CHICKIE: . . . OK.

CHARLIE: . . . OK. Go get the pizza now.

CHICKIE: Charlie?

CHARLIE: Yeah?

CHICKIE: Do you think you could show my boyfriend how to be a Jedi? Me and him, we're supposed to go to Baltimore to see his friend Jon Seda the TV and movie actor, and maybe you could come too, and you could teach him how to be a Jedi, and maybe Jon Seda, he might wanna be one too, but mostly, you could teach my boyfriend 'cuz he'd prolly be good like you if you taught him. Could you do that?

CHARLIE: I don't know.

CHICKIE: Why not?

CHARLIE: 'Cuz my doctor over there at the place, he said that to be a Jedi fighter, you can't lie, steal, and you can't do drugs ever.

CHICKIE: Oh. *(Beat.)* I think I'll go get the pizza now.

CHARLIE: OK.

CHICKIE: You want three Yoohoos to drink, right?

CHARLIE: Uhhuh.

CHICKIE: I'm gonna get a Diet Shasta, OK?

CHARLIE: Yeah.

CHICKIE: Can I get some gum for me and some of those little chocolate donuts for my boyfriend?

CHARLIE: OK.

CHICKIE: Have you seen my boyfriend today?

CHARLIE: Nah.

CHICKIE: OK.

CHARLIE: Chickie?

CHICKIE: What?

CHARLIE: . . . Nuttin'.

CHICKIE: OK. *(Chickie exits.)*

# Jesus Hopped the A Train
## Stephen Adly Guirgis

*Dramatic*

Angel (twenties) and Mary Jane (late twenties to late thirties)

> *Angel is an incarcerated Hispanic man. Mary Jane is his court-appointed attorney.*
>
> *Manhattan Correctional Center, legal consultations room. Mary Jane and Angel (beaten up) midstream:*

ANGEL: — What I want is a fuckin' lawyer!! Is it possible, in this nightmare — I mean, what the fuck is this?! — Even on TV they get a lawyer —

MARY JANE: I am a lawyer, I'm your lawyer —

ANGEL: I wanna real lawyer!

MARY JANE: I am a real lawyer, and you are my real client —

ANGEL: Fuck that!

MARY JANE: You wanna see the paperwork?

ANGEL: Fuck the paperwork! Why didn't you check the paperwork before you came in here talkin all kinda shit when you didn't even know who you was speakin' to?

MARY JANE: Look, I am sorry for the mix-up, I —

ANGEL: The "mix-up"? Is that what happened before? Or do you just never know who anybody is?

MARY JANE: I'm sorry!

ANGEL: I ain't Hector Villanueva!!

MARY JANE: I know that —

ANGEL: Hector Villanueva, No Aqui!!

MARY JANE: OK, what I need from you —

ANGEL: Need?! You gonna sit there and talk to me about what you need? I'm incarcerated, lady! Why can't we talk about what I fuckin need?!

MARY JANE: What do you need?

ANGEL: I need a damn lawyer!!!

MARY JANE: Which is why I'm here —

ANGEL: This is bullshit! This is racism is what it is, racism!! If I was white, I'd have motherfuckin' Perry Mason sittin here wit the little glasses and the beard talkin fuckin' strategy. Instead they give me some bumblin'-ass Wilma Flintstone don't even know who I am!!

MARY JANE: You are Angel Cruz, you are thirty years old, you live with your mom on Tiemen Place, West Harlem. You have one felony prior, a robbery, you were sixteen. You work as a bike messenger. You had a year of college, you played soccer —

ANGEL: I never played soccer!!

MARY JANE: You're charged with Attempted Murder, I know that.

ANGEL: Attempted Murder??!! —

MARY JANE: — That surprises you? —

ANGEL: — Ya see bitch? Dass exactly what I'm talkin 'bout! All I did —

MARY JANE: — Stop!

ANGEL: All I did was shoot him in the ass, what the fuck is "attempted murder" about that, huh?! . . . Stupid ass! . . . What??!!

*(Mary Jane rises, begins collecting her things.)*

What are you doing?

MARY JANE: I'm leaving.

ANGEL: Why, 'cuz I called you a bitch?

MARY JANE: No, because you just confessed to me.

ANGEL: Confessed? Confessed what?

MARY JANE: You just admitted to me that you did the shooting.

ANGEL: No I didn't!

MARY JANE: You just said, "All I did was shoot him in the ass."

ANGEL: So?

MARY JANE: So now you get your wish: I can't adequately defend you now, so you'll get another lawyer.

ANGEL: What if I don't want another lawyer?

MARY JANE: You just got through haranguing me —

ANGEL: "Haranguing"?

MARY JANE: Haranguing: It means —

ANGEL: I know what the fuck it means. Whaddya think? I'm a Puerto Rican, therefore I'm a motherfuckah who can't know shit?

MARY JANE: Yeah, that's exactly what I was thinking —

ANGEL: I know a lot a fuckin' shit!

MARY JANE: Well then know this: When the next lawyer walks in here, tomorrow, or the day after, try not to confess to him —

ANGEL: Tomorrow??!! —

MARY JANE: Because when you confess to your lawyer, Angel, it means we can't put you on the witness stand —

ANGEL: — Hold up —

MARY JANE: Because if we did put you on the witness stand, we would be suborning perjury and I'm sure, of course, that you know what "suborning" means, but on the off chance you might've missed that vocabulary word during your high school years at Power Memorial, let me refresh you: It means if you're lying up there, we can't know about it —

ANGEL: OK —

MARY JANE: — And if we do know about it, we're obligated to inform the court —

ANGEL: So —

MARY JANE: — And if we don't inform the court and someone finds out about it, then we get in a lot of trouble!

ANGEL: If you had tol' me this shit before —

MARY JANE: And another thing: If a public defender confuses you with someone else, it might be because they have dozens of other cases and they made an honest mistake! This is the criminal justice system you're in now. Mix-ups happen here! —

ANGEL: — So whatchu gonna do about it?!

MARY JANE: What am I gonna do? —

ANGEL: — 'Cuz I ain't got till tomorrow —

MARY JANE: Lemme give you a little tip: The trick, Angel, is not to have a lawyer who makes no mistakes, but to get the lawyer who (A) makes the least mistakes and (B) is either green enough or masochistic enough to actually give a shit about their clients.

ANGEL: So which one are you?

MARY JANE: I'm neither. *(Mary Jane exits. Blackout.)*

# Late Night in the Womens' Restroom in the Jungle Bar

David Riedy

Comic

Ben and Haley (twenties to thirties)

*Haley has fled her ostensibly happy home and husband and come to a local bar looking for a friend who can take her in, at least for the night. Her husband, Ben, comes to find out what's wrong.*

HALEY: What do you want? Ben — put your hand down.

BEN: This note — *(Pulls out note from pocket.)* — you left.

HALEY: I did.

BEN: You left? You're leaving? Me?

HALEY: How did you know I was here?

BEN: Someone called. Told me. Said she was a friend and she was worried about you. I have been up all night, calling everywhere for you. I was just about to call the police —

HALEY: What do you want?

BEN: You just leave this note and disappear?

HALEY: What do you want?

BEN: I want you to come home.

HALEY: Why?

BEN: So we can talk about this.

HALEY: Go ahead: talk.

BEN: Let's do this at home. Please.

HALEY: Why?

BEN: Because it's two in the morning and I just ran across town and am standing in the women's restroom of some dive bar talking to my wife who's in a little black dress I've never seen before! This is embarrassing. I am exhausted. Come home.

HALEY: There is a man out there who thinks my name is Heather and who says he has 100 reasons why I should let him take me home and have dirty filthy sweaty smelly sex with me. He said he wants to make electric currents pulse through my body until I'm writhing on the bed in ecstasy — I'd be the socket and he'd be the plug!

*(Beat.)*

BEN: OK . . .

HALEY: Why shouldn't I go home with him?

BEN: You're not making any sense. Are you drunk? You always get irrational when you're drunk.

HALEY: I am very rational right now.

BEN: Come on, Haley, let's go home and we can talk about this in the morning —

HALEY: This can't wait until morning!

BEN: *(Calmly:)* Then we'll talk about it tonight. But not here.

HALEY: What if I should go home with him?

BEN: What do you mean "should"? You should come home with me. You're my wife.

HALEY: Not right now. In this restroom right now, in my head I'm not. I'm nobody. I'm homeless. I am a woman without a home, a ship without a harbor, a — a car with no garage.

BEN: Haley —

HALEY: I don't know who I am: Haley or Heather.

BEN: You're Haley. My wife. You know that. You're just unhappy and mad —

HALEY: I'M NOT "JUST!" DON'T "JUST" ME, BEN! I am a lot more than just unhappy and mad. I am questioning tonight. I'm questioning me. I'm questioning you. I'm questioning us.

BEN: Did something happen —

HALEY: I have a question for you.

BEN: What?

HALEY: "What is love?"

BEN: I don't want to, but —

HALEY: OK, OK — that's kind of broad. "What is the right way to love someone?"

BEN: I will carry you out of here if I have to.

HALEY: How about "Why should I go back to being the ugly old wife in our boring old marriage when there are perfectly good brand-new men out there willing to love me for who I want to be for however long I want to be it? What does three years mean, anyway?" Tell me, Ben.

*(Beat.)*

BEN: You're testing me — !

HALEY: Answer the question.

BEN: — comparing the Christmas presents I get you with the ones your sister got from her boyfriend, asking if I remember that August fifteenth — !

HALEY: Answer the question.

BEN: — is the day we first kissed in public, standing on a street corner. And if I remember that you want to know what street corner!

HALEY: ANSWER THE QUESTION!

BEN: WHICH ONE!!?!

HALEY: ALL OF THEM! Any of them.

BEN: I can't, Haley. I can't. They're impossible to answer, because you're the only one with the answers. Tell me what you want me to say, and I'll say it. I'll say whatever you want.

HALEY: I want you to tell me why I should keep loving you.

BEN: Because I'm so irresistible you can't help yourself.

HALEY: I mean it.

BEN: I can't tell you that either, Haley. I can only stand here and tell you that three years is not a long time. It's not. My parents have been together for thirty-five years. And I know that your parents didn't stay together — .

HALEY: Don't bring my parents into this.

BEN: OK. OK.

HALEY: You don't listen. You don't . . . this is serious.

BEN: I know it is. We'll talk about it tomorrow. Come home.

*(Ben reaches his hand out to Haley. Beat. She takes her wedding ring out of her bra and puts it in his hand. Beat.)*

BEN: What does this mean?

HALEY: Hold on to that for me for a while. I'm not sure if it fits anymore.

*(Ben looks at the ring.)*

BEN: What is happening here?

HALEY: I have to know for sure, before —

BEN: Know what?

HALEY: If — I'm only part of myself when I'm with you. I don't know if I want to let the other part of me go, yet.

*(Long pause.)*

BEN: So . . . I should go?

HALEY: Yes.

# Mooncalf
## Elizabeth Karlin

*Dramatic*

Miranda and Donald (teens)

> *This play takes place in a hospital. Miranda is a cranky girl, borderline troubled, whose mother has cancer and is in the hospital. On a visit to her mother, she meets Donald, who's a cancer patient himself. In this scene, they discover that they have a lot in common.*

> *A hallway. Miranda and Donald come from opposite directions. He is wearing pajamas and a bathrobe. He pulls along an IV pole. She is carrying a bag from a stationery store. He tries to pass, but she blocks him and the music stops.*

MIRANDA: Hey . . . Donald?

DONALD: *(Looking at the floor.)* Oh . . . hi.

MIRANDA: Remember me . . . Miranda . . . From the other day?

DONALD: Yea.

> *(He starts to go but Miranda grabs his pole.)*

MIRANDA: Hold on . . . what is all this? Are you a patient here?

DONALD: What does it look like?

MIRANDA: You have cancer?

DONALD: Uh-huh.

MIRANDA: My God. I'm speechless. I am like so totally speechless. I don't know what to say. I thought you were just hanging around, like me, for some relative or something. You didn't look like a patient so how was I supposed to know? Why didn't you say something? You know you should tell somebody something like that . . . somebody you're talking to. You sit there and you don't say a word about it? What's that about? You should let somebody know so they don't say something stupid. I must've sounded really . . . Wow. I'm absolutely speechless.

DONALD: I'm sorry.

MIRANDA: It's OK but don't do that again. It is totally rude. So what do you have, exactly?

DONALD: Hodgkins.

MIRANDA: Oh, that's the best kind.

DONALD: It is?

MIRANDA: Oh yea, lots of kids get that and they get over it. It's the best kind of cancer to have, really.

DONALD: Can you let go of my pole?

MIRANDA: Why?

DONALD: I have to go.

MIRANDA: Why do you always have to go? You don't like me very much, do you?

DONALD: I didn't say . . .

MIRANDA: That's OK. I don't care what people think about me.

DONALD: I'm going to my room.

MIRANDA: Where's your room?

DONALD: Down the hall.

MIRANDA: My mother's on the other side. Your friends come and see you?

DONALD: Friends?

MIRANDA: Yea, friends . . . you know, your compadres . . . amigos . . .

DONALD: Uh . . . no.

MIRANDA: Are you an only child?

DONALD: I'm not lonely.

MIRANDA: I said only . . . brothers, sisters?

DONALD: Oh. No, I don't have any.

MIRANDA: Me neither. We have a lot in common. I almost had a brother but he was born dead. My mom's like bipolar. You know what that is?

DONALD: Not really.

MIRANDA: She's one of those people who like, when she's sad she's impossible and when she's happy she's worse. You never know which it's going to be . . . And sometimes she sings . . . *(Miranda shudders.)*

I think that Ben . . . that was going to be his name . . . got wind of what he'd be in for and did the sensible thing by choking himself with the umbilical cord. *(Miranda punctuates that by firmly pulling an imaginary cord around her neck.)* He showed her. I don't know, sometimes I think it's me, that I wasn't born to have parents. What does your mom do?

DONALD: She's a secretary.

MIRANDA: You mean like in an office? So she must be away all day. And if you have no friends or anything you must get like really bored here. I'll keep you company, if you want.

DONALD: That's OK.

MIRANDA: I don't mind. I just have to deliver this stuff to my mother. You need a pencil? I got a million of them here — all sharpened. I'm not going to even tell you what she needs them for, it's too weird.

DONALD: I have to go. There's a movie on TV . . .

MIRANDA: Oh yea? What movie?

DONALD: Nothing you ever heard of.

MIRANDA: How do you know?

DONALD: It's an old movie.

MIRANDA: You mean like *The Godfather?*

DONALD: No, a really old movie.

MIRANDA: What's the name of it?

DONALD: *Fallen Angel.*

MIRANDA: I saw that.

DONALD: You did?

MIRANDA: Sure. It's about some skanky girl who runs away from Minnesota and winds up . . .

DONALD: No! This is directed by Otto Preminger.

MIRANDA: Oh.

DONALD: Do you know who Otto Preminger is?

MIRANDA: I know the name. So who's in the movie?

DONALD: Dana Andrews.

MIRANDA: Who's she?

DONALD: *(Exasperated.)* He's a man!

MIRANDA: Oh. So is there anybody famous in this movie? Like somebody I might have actually heard of?

DONALD: All the regular Twentieth Century Fox players — Linda Darnell, Alice Faye . . .

MIRANDA: Are they guys too?

DONALD: . . . John Carradine, Anne Revere, Jimmy Conlin, Charles Bickford, Bruce Cabot, Percy Kilbride . . .

MIRANDA: Oh my God, you're one of those.

DONALD: What?

MIRANDA: You know, with the movie trivia. There's a whole bunch of you boys skulking around out there, holed up in dark rooms, living in a past that's not even your own.

DONALD: I'm not . . .

MIRANDA: I live in the here and now. You should meet my mother. She's into that shit, big time. She stays up all night watching old, decrepit black-and-white movies. She's always trying to get me to join her but the truth is that I hate movies.

DONALD: You hate movies?

MIRANDA: I can't stand them. They're so artificial and cliché. "I love you, I love you, I love you." Who talks like that? And people sit around and watch that shit? I'm a doer not a watcher.

DONALD: Yea, well . . .

MIRANDA: I read books. That's where I get my entertainment.

DONALD: *(He starts on his way.)* I gotta go.

MIRANDA: *(She grabs the pole again.)* I'll watch it with you.

DONALD: I thought you're not a watcher.

MIRANDA: I don't mind.

DONALD: Maybe another time. Can you let go of my pole, please?

MIRANDA: I'll let go, on one condition.

DONALD: What?

MIRANDA: After the movie you come and get me at my mother's room.

DONALD: Why?

MIRANDA: You'll be saving my life. It'll be like a rescue. You can rescue me like . . . like you're . . .

DONALD: Errol Flynn?

MIRANDA: Yea, him. Come rescue me like you're Errol Flynn and I'll owe you one.

DONALD: I don't know . . .

MIRANDA: Oh come on, please.

DONALD: Maybe.

MIRANDA: It's room 1219 . . . *(She releases the pole.)* Don't forget me now, 'cause I know where to find you.

*(Miranda goes on her way, swinging the bag. Donald goes on his way in the opposite direction, a smile slowly forming on his face.)*

# More Lies About Jerzy
## Davey Holmes

*Seriocomic*

Jerzy (forties) and Georgia (younger)

> *This play is a fascinating fictionalized account of the last days of the Pol-*
> *ish novelist Jerzy Kozinski. In this scene Jerzy and Georgia discuss an*
> *article being written about Jerzy by Georgia's boss. She is a fact-checker,*
> *and she has some intriguing questions to ask him.*

JERZY: I walk into the office and she recognizes me.

GEORGIA: Mr Lesnewski!

JERZY: Her name is . . . Jean.

GEORGIA: I'm Georgia.

JERZY: Jean is at her desk . . .

GEORGIA: We met a few weeks ago.

JERZY: Oh yes! I was with Paul and —

GEORGIA: I brought you a sandwich. Which isn't my job.

JERZY: I hope I didn't . . .

GEORGIA: No, I mean . . . I wanted to. I was getting one for myself anyway. I just meant, if I had to do it, it wouldn't have been much of a
gesture, so . . .
*(She trails off, hating herself. Jerzy smiles.)*

JERZY: I'm looking for Arthur Bausley. I went to his office, they sent me
here.

GEORGIA: Is this about the article? Conflicting dates . . . ?

JERZY: *(Suspicious.)* Yes . . .

GEORGIA: I've been working with Arthur. Checking facts. Which actually is my job.

JERZY: Ah. So you have a list of the . . . "inconsistencies"?

GEORGIA: Arthur will want to be the one who . . .

JERZY: *(Holds a hand out.)* Please.

*(Georgia hesitates, then hands him a page. She waits nervously while he reads.)*

JERZY: *"When was he separated from his parents?"* The only one who can tell you that is me. You have to take my word.

GEORGIA: Except, in your biography —

JERZY: The bio is wrong. These dates are right. Eh? I make your job easy.

GEORGIA: I guess.

*(Jerzy looks at her for a moment.)*

JERZY: You're very beautiful. *(Pause.)* So, we're done here?

GEORGIA: I . . . those are the only questions we . . .

JERZY: I won't bother you further. *(He starts out.)*

GEORGIA: Actually — Arthur should be back in a minute. If you don't mind . . .

JERZY: No . . .

*(Jerzy takes a seat. A pause.)*

GEORGIA: It's great to . . . really meet you. I've been thinking about you and your writing . . .

JERZY: You've been thinking about me?

GEORGIA: Well, I don't know you. The book . . .

JERZY: *(Pointing.)* Is that your copy?

GEORGIA: Yes.

JERZY: Would you like me to sign it?

GEORGIA: I —

JERZY: Don't answer that. Sometimes I catch a glimpse of my ego, like the shadow of some huge, flapping —

GEORGIA: *(Holding book.)* I'd appreciate it.

JERZY: Pen?

*(She hands him the book and a pen.)*

JERZY: *(Writing.)* "Dear . . ."?

GEORGIA: Georgia.

JERZY: " — Georgia. I will never forget our time together. These last years have been one long . . . sexual . . . whirlwind. Love, Jerzy." *(Hands it back.)*

GEORGIA: That will confuse the biographers.

JERZY: Mine or yours?

GEORGIA: I don't think anyone's going to write about me. I'm happier spying on other people.

JERZY: You look in their windows.

GEORGIA: I research. People with extraordinary lives. In your case . . . what you went through in the war, and in this country. Coming here with nothing and now you're famous —

JERZY: Not so extraordinary. Anyone can do this, if they Exploit the Moment.

*(Georgia waits for him to explain. Jerzy's chair is on coasters; he shoves off and coasts over to her.)*

JERZY: Always, even as a child, I felt an obligation to control each second as a dramatic unit. You understand?

GEORGIA: No.

JERZY: To analyze every situation as honestly as possible, then build on it.

GEORGIA: For example . . .

*(Jerzy considers.)*

JERZY: You and I are waiting. We don't know each other. You're worried about my "inconsistencies," maybe you're a threat. But I find you attractive. I launch into a pretentious, semi-intellectual rant which is meant to impress you. Maybe you find it flattering, maybe you're suspicious. What do I want? Is it something you want to give?

GEORGIA: So we . . . boil it down to . . .

JERZY: Usually it's instinctive. But for the purpose of discussion, this moment is about . . . ? *(Pause.)*

GEORGIA: Curiosity.

JERZY: Ah!

GEORGIA: I just mean, I've been reading your book, so —

JERZY: We have an obligation to curiosity. To surrender to it. Drown in it. And one course of action which comes to mind —

*(The phone rings.)*

GEORGIA: Probably Arthur.

*(Jerzy leans back, and she has to reach around him to answer it.)*

GEORGIA: Georgia speaking. What? No, she's already left. *(Makes a note.)* All right.

*(Jerzy now has the cradle of the phone in his lap. Georgia pauses before hanging up.)*

GEORGIA: You were saying?

JERZY: *(Cavalier now.)* You get the idea.

GEORGIA: What if the moment already is what it is? Why do you want to make it more?

JERZY: Possibly I need to compensate for my own inadequacy.

GEORGIA: What inadequacy?

JERZY: I don't want to burden you with . . .

GEORGIA: No, go ahead.

*(Jerzy takes a deep breath.)*

JERZY: When I was young, I was attacked by a group of children. There was a little girl . . . You know this from my book.

*(Georgia nods.)*

JERZY: What you don't know is . . . they left me damaged. *(Then.)* They took a stick. And did things . . . *(Then.)* . . . to my penis.

GEORGIA: Oh . . . !

*(Beat.)*

JERZY: Have I upset you?

GEORGIA: I'm . . . that's very . . .

JERZY: You feel repulsed?

GEORGIA: Not at all.

JERZY: Curious?

GEORGIA: *(Pause.)* Is it true?

JERZY: *(Getting up.)* What do you mean, "Is it true" — ? *(Quickly.)* Come have a drink with me.

GEORGIA: When?

JERZY: Now.

GEORGIA: I have to work. Otherwise I . . . I'd love to, but —

JERZY: Can I use your phone? *(Dials a number.)* Hello, Paul? Jerzy. I'm working with a research assistant of yours, Georgia . . . ?

GEORGIA: Fischer.

JERZY: *(Into phone.)* Georgia Fischer. Mind if I borrow her for a while? I'll return her in roughly the same condition. Thanks. *(Hangs up.)* Get your coat.

GEORGIA: We're going out.

JERZY: Yes.

GEORGIA: Because . . . we have an obligation to . . .

JERZY: Exactly.

*(Light on Georgia.)*

GEORGIA: When he wrote about me he used the name Jean. Outside of that he didn't change much. The first night we had dinner then went to his apartment. And his penis was fine so . . . I guess it was a joke. Or something.

# Platonically Incorrect

## Darlene Hunt

*Comic*

Steve and Darlene (twenties to thirties)

> *Darlene and Steve are friends. In this scene, Darlene tells Steve about a guy she is now dating who has unusual sexual tastes.*

> *Loud party music. Steve and Darlene dance wildly behind a scrim in silhouette. When the song ends, they stumble breathlessly onto the balcony holding beers. Party music plays low in the background.*

STEVE: So tell me about this guy you're seeing.

DARLENE: He's good. It's good. He's good. He's different.

STEVE: Different like I'm different?

DARLENE: No baby, you're crazy. He's just different from other guys I've dated. He's a little . . .

STEVE: What?

DARLENE: A little . . .

STEVE: A little what?

DARLENE: Just a little . . . Hispanic.

STEVE: Oh, D, that's good.

DARLENE: I know. Right? Little girl from Kentucky all grown up and embracing diversity.

STEVE: So that's good.

    *(Beat.)*

DARLENE: There's something else.

STEVE: Yep. I felt it.

DARLENE: He's into smells.

STEVE: Smells?

DARLENE: Yep.

STEVE: We're not talking incense here, are we? Wood grain? Raspberry?

DARLENE: Nope.

STEVE: Body odor?

DARLENE: Yeah, sure, and there's more.

*(Steve braces himself for this new information.)*

STEVE: Mmm. Hmm. I'm not ready.

DARLENE: Let me know.

STEVE: OK, give me a second.

DARLENE: Take your time.

*(Beat.)*

STEVE: OK now.

DARLENE: He likes a smelly pussy.

STEVE: OK, I'm walkin'.

*(Steve walks in circles and breathes deeply.)*

DARLENE: Walk it out. It's a tough one.

*(They finally come together.)*

DARLENE: So is he aberrant or is this a thing?

STEVE: It's a thing.

DARLENE: It is?

STEVE: It's not *my* thing but yes it is a thing.

DARLENE: I had no idea.

STEVE: It's gonna be hard for you.

DARLENE: I know.

STEVE: 'Cause you're a clean freak.

DARLENE: I know. I know.

STEVE: But it could be good.

DARLENE: Fewer showers. It could save a lot of time.

STEVE: More time for . . . you know.

DARLENE: Oh, I know.

*(The dance music gets louder.)*

# Praying for Rain
## Robert Lewis Vaughan

*Dramatic*

Marc and Erin (late teens)

> *Marc, formerly a star high school athlete, has had a terrible motorcycle accident in which he almost died. Because he can no longer play sports he has lost his sense of self, and nobody else seems to be able to relate to him. In this scene, he confronts Erin, a former friend, wanting to know why she has been avoiding him.*

MARC: Hey. HEY! *(Pause.)* Hey Erin!
    *(A moment and Erin, dressed in running clothes, trots onstage.)*
ERIN: What?
MARC: I just, you know, wanted to say you looked good out there.
ERIN: Thanks. *(She starts off.)*
MARC: That's it? Why won't you talk to me anymore?
ERIN: Sorry. I'm kinda . . . How's your back?
MARC: It's fine. My knees are still all fucked up but . . . you know.
ERIN: Are you gonna be able to play again?
MARC: Probably not. It's OK though.
ERIN: Why do you say that? You were —
MARC: It's no big deal. I mean, it's not like —
ERIN: Whatever, I gotta — *(She starts off again.)*
MARC: So, like, since I don't play anymore you can't talk to me?
ERIN: . . . No . . .
MARC: Yeah, right.
ERIN: Where's Chris and Jim?
MARC: Why?
ERIN: It's too early to be out rolling drunks on McMasters and lately I haven't seen you without them lurking somewhere nearby. So . . .
MARC: They're all right.

ERIN: They're criminals.

MARC: No they aren't.

ERIN: Bullshit, Marc.

MARC: They don't roll drunks either.

ERIN: Janet Vasquez told me they got busted a month ago for trying to roll some drunk guy outside the Baby Doll.

MARC: Once.

ERIN: Yeah, right.

MARC: So . . . I wasn't there, I didn't do anything.

ERIN: Yet.

MARC: What's that supposed to mean?

ERIN: You hang out with them too much. Ever since you got in that accident, you . . . It's like you don't care about anything. You don't . . .

MARC: What else is there to do around this place? It's not like I can —

ERIN: Whatever, Marc. I gotta —

MARC: Wait. Don't go yet.

ERIN: What?

MARC: Nothing. I just . . . *(He lights another cigarette using his first.)*

ERIN: I'm really sorry, Marc.

MARC: Really? Why?

ERIN: That's another thing. It's like you dare people to not like you anymore. You're like, acting like you're all that, and you never did that before. Were you just waiting for me so you could —

MARC: I wasn't doing anything. I like watching you run. I really —

ERIN: Yeah?

MARC: No.

ERIN: You make me sad.

MARC: Why's that?

ERIN: You died after you — I mean . . . You almost died . . .

MARC: Well, I didn't really —

ERIN: Almost.

MARC: I guess.

ERIN: Were you scared?

MARC: Yeah, I guess. When I knew. I didn't know until I wasn't gonna die that I almost died. So. It was kinda like . . . well I'm not but I almost did . . . so.

ERIN: Nobody in my family's even dead yet. Well, my great-grampa died before I was born, but great-gramma's like really old. My mom says she's not gonna die until my uncle gets to be Pope. He's a monsignor at the Vatican.

MARC: Really?

ERIN: Yeah. He's nice.

MARC: I don't have any famous relatives. I don't even feel like I have relatives.

ERIN: He isn't famous. What do you mean?

MARC: Nobody in my family even talks really and I don't remember any of our other relatives.

ERIN: Your dad's your stepdad, right?

MARC: Yeah. My real dad's . . . he never comes around.

ERIN: Where is he now?

MARC: I think he's in California or someplace like that.

ERIN: Do you miss him?

MARC: I don't really know him, and . . . you know . . . my stepdad, so . . .

ERIN: He and your mom still fight?

MARC: Sometimes. I just leave. You know. Whatever.

ERIN: People don't really make fun of your mom, you know. I know you're all embarrassed and stuff, and think people laugh at you, but they don't. You should just —

MARC: — Whatever . . . you don't really know what it's —

ERIN: Well . . . I should . . . *(She starts out again.)*

MARC: Erin, wait. Please? I'm . . .

*(She stops.)*

MARC: Do you wanna maybe . . . hang out . . . sometime . . . or something . . . ?

ERIN: . . . well . . . I'm. I'm kinda going out with . . .

MARC: . . . yeah . . .

ERIN: I think your boys are coming this way . . . *(She looks off; he turns.)*

MARC: . . . I mean, just to hang out. Not like anything . . . you know . . .

ERIN: Yeah. Sure . . . *(She starts off.)* See ya, Marc. *(She's gone.)*

# Quake
## Melanie Marnich

*Comic*

Lucy (twenties to thirties) and Man (same age or a little older)

> *This very inventive comedy is about Lucy, a single woman in search of Mr. Right. In the play she tried various men on for size before moving on to the next encounter. In this encounter, she meets a sweaty auto mechanic who offers something she hasn't tried yet — violent, abusive sex. Some girls like it rough. Maybe Lucy's one of those girls.*

> *Somewhere in the West. Lucy enters an auto repair garage, fresh from her fairly recent visit to the sexy club. There is a dangerously good-looking man slouched there.*

LUCY: Hello.

MAN: Hep.

LUCY: This is a . . . garage?

MAN: Yep.

LUCY: And you are a . . . mechanic?

MAN: Uhn.

LUCY: I like your . . . tools.

MAN: Mmn.

LUCY: When I was growing up, there was this neighbor-guy. He spent all his time in his garage with his car. He was either under the hood or under the whole thing, rolling around on his back on this little roly cart. And he never talked. Not a word. He was amazing and had great stomach muscles. He had a big black tool box. He was like a grease monkey James Dean. Or Dennis Quaid. You are just like he was. And he was so hot. I always wanted one like him. I can't believe I just said that. Pretend I didn't say that. Act like I didn't say that. I didn't say that. I didn't. Oh God. *(She pats her forehead and face with a handkerchief.)* Oh God. Can I start over? I'm starting over. Brand new. OK. Um, hello.

MAN: Hep.

LUCY: This is a . . . garage?

MAN: Yep.

LUCY: And you are a . . . mechanic?

MAN: Uhn.

LUCY: My car's broken.

MAN: Hmph.

LUCY: It just petered out.

> *(Man lights a cigarette.)*

LUCY: At first I thought it was just me, but then the warning lights started coming on. And it smelled.

> *(Man smokes.)*

LUCY: Yeah, so I got it off the freeway because some of the dials were going into the red warning danger-danger zone. I thought it was gonna, you know, blow.

> *(Man smokes.)*

LUCY: Like, blow up.

> *(Man smokes.)*

LUCY: With me in it. So I got out. Got a tow. And here I am. So um. What do you think?

> *(Man thinks. And thinks.)*

MAN: Sounds like a carburetor/crankshaft/hose/joint/nut/bolt/spark/fuel/bullshit/crap thing.

LUCY: You talk!

MAN: Of course I talk.

LUCY: I didn't think guys like you talk!

MAN: Make too big a deal out of it, and I'll stop.

LUCY: Sorry.

MAN: Stick to car stuff, and we'll be fine.

LUCY: OK. So. In terms of car stuff, when will it be ready? My car.

MAN: Won't get started on it till tomorrow.

LUCY: Oh.

MAN: Or the day after.

LUCY: I can't go anywhere till you fix it.

MAN: I know.

LUCY: I know you know. You're the expert.

MAN: You like that, don't you? That I'm the expert.

LUCY: Yes.

MAN: With cars.

LUCY: I guess so.

MAN: You do. You like that I know cars but don't know much else. And that you think rings around me and talk circles around me and know big words and big books and big things and I have a tenth grade education. And that I look good in a pair of jeans.

LUCY: Just something about a guy with grease under his nails. Who smells like gasoline and cigarettes and who knows what to do with a belt sander.

MAN: You like that?

LUCY: Oh yeah.

*(Man stares at her.)*

LUCY: It's. Manly. Intensely. Manly.

MAN: And you like the way I hold my beer bottle by its neck. You like that I sit in the chair in the kitchen, quiet, because that's just me being strong. And silent. Because silence is sexy. *(Silence.)* Because silence is electricity. Because silence is intensity. Because you can fill the quiet with whatever you want me to be. Like they do in the pretty movies. Because isn't it great that a girl like you and a guy like me can — Well. Isn't it . . . romantic?

*(But it's not romantic. It's sinister.)*

LUCY: Are you ready to work on my — ?

MAN: I'm just getting started.

LUCY: Could you . . . hurry?

MAN: No.

LUCY: Oh.

MAN: And you want one like me because . . . ?

LUCY: Because . . .

MAN: And you want me why . . . ?

LUCY: Well . . .

MAN: Because I scare you. And that's why you'll lay down for me.

Because I'm rough, I won't play nice. And you want it that way, don't you?

You know I know how to kiss in a way that takes the air out of your joints. You know I'll put one finger inside you, then two, then five, then my fist, up to my elbow, my shoulder, my head is inside, I'm going upstream and pretty soon I'm doing the Australian crawl through your bloodstream.

And nobody's done that to you before.

You always wanted one like me. And I'm not nice.

*(He's maneuvered her onto her back on the floor. He's crouched over her, on all fours.)*

LUCY: Are you gonna hit me?

MAN: I'm gonna knock your socks off.

LUCY: You gonna hurt me?

MAN: Don't worry. After a while, it'll just make you smell different. And that's how I'll find you. How I'll always know where you are. By your smell.

LUCY: Bruises?

MAN: They're just the flowers your body gives you for taking the punch. *(He crawls around her.)* I'll bounce you off the side of the pickup truck, and you'll know I love you. I'll fuck you up the ass till you spit out your teeth and you'll know I'm crazy for you.

*(He moves down to her feet and starts to smell her, still on all fours, working his way up her body as she starts to cry. He passes over her, a knee on each side of her body, so that he's like a cage over her. He's gone. She lies there.)*

# Sheridan, or Schooled in Scandal

## David Grimm

*Seriocomic*

Lord Byron (twenties) and Duchess of Devonshire (older)

> *This comic drama is about Richard Brinsley Sheridan (his life and times).
> In this scene, the Duchess of Devonshire has invited Byron to her home
> to discuss a business offer and, possibly, blackmail him.*

> *A terrace off the Duchess of Devonshire's apartments. Late afternoon sun.
> The sounds of stringed instruments mixed with the whispered chatter of
> women and the fluttering of fans from the next room. A man in his early
> twenties, dressed recklessly. His hair is wild. He walks with a limp: Byron.*

BYRON: London. Back in time for autumn. In time to entertain the rich
and illiterate in their own homes. Bottles of port. Forced smiles. The
latest fashion. Numbing. The smell of winter coming. Sunsets get
sadder and more elegant. Still, darkness. Candles. Dust. *(Pause; he
breathes.)* Yet another literary salon.
*(The Duchess of Devonshire appears with a drink. A very well dressed
woman of a certain age. Elegant. Cultured.)*

DEVONSHIRE: Lord Byron, you're alone. We thought you'd left us.

BYRON: I needed to take the air.

DEVONSHIRE: We found your poem . . . invigorating.

BYRON: A few of the ladies looked faint. I thought they'd shit themselves.

DEVONSHIRE: We are not accustomed to your sort of —

BYRON: Honesty?

DEVONSHIRE: Confrontation. Pity you're not published. Print has a way
of making men seem almost respectable. May I offer you a drink?
*(Byron is served a drink.)*

DEVONSHIRE: Three years in Turkey and Greece have done much for you.

BYRON: Three years have done little for London society. It's as small-minded as ever.

DEVONSHIRE: I must admit, I have never been particularly fond of poetry. This need for metaphor — frankly, it's tiresome. However, it is fashionable these days to admire a well-turned verse or a capering couplet and, being a woman of mode, I must embrace the current style. I have never cared much for men, either. But I do appreciate what they represent. Tell me, what does a young man such as yourself aspire to most?

BYRON: What any young man aspires to. Fortune, fame, fornication. Do I shock you?

DEVONSHIRE: I am far too rich to be shocked. In fact, I can place these aspirations within your reach. I can hand you your dreams like a bottle of port and you can drink all you like.

BYRON: The profit of dreams is best earned and not purchased, Your Grace. What is the Duchess of Devonshire after?

DEVONSHIRE: Power. That is what men represent. I would like to publish one of your poems. The one you read tonight. It's very new.

BYRON: The latest fashion?

DEVONSHIRE: Lord Byron, let me be blunt. I did not invite you to my home solely to recite your little masterpiece. I invited you to discuss a business transaction.

BYRON: Serving up my poems in today's conservative climate doesn't show very sound business sense. I fail to see the point.

DEVONSHIRE: You will. Tell me, how well do you know Mister Sheridan?

BYRON: Richard Brinsley Sheridan? The man is only our greatest living writer for the stage and a highly respected member of Parliament.

DEVONSHIRE: I did not ask for his credentials, but I ask if you do know him.

BYRON: *The Rivals* — *School for Scandal* — I've read and witnessed every play he ever wrote. The man's a genius.

DEVONSHIRE: Be that as it may, this genius has involved himself in a very dangerous enterprise. His theater, the Drury Lane, has fallen upon hard times. In attempting to maintain its solvency, he has turned to the Prince of Wales for financial support.

BYRON: There is nothing dangerous about royal patronage.

DEVONSHIRE: In exchange for these moneys, Mister Sheridan has been arranging assignations for the prince. He has procured for him a Mrs. Maria Fitzherbert — a woman of low birth. An army widow. And a Catholic.

BYRON: I have no interest in malicious gossip, Your Grace. If you'll excuse me —

DEVONSHIRE: The prince has, for lack of better words, fallen in love with the woman. Sheridan has been transporting their letters. Acting as their secret messenger.

BYRON: The private dealings between discreet persons are of no concern to me or anyone.

DEVONSHIRE: Ah, but you're wrong. The private is political, Lord Byron. And the future of our royal house cannot be toyed with by the likes of Mister Sheridan. Such an affair cannot be allowed to continue.

BYRON: What is this matter to me?

DEVONSHIRE: I want you to intercept their letters.

BYRON: *(Pause; laughing.)* You hold the most intriguing salons, Your Grace. I bid you a good night.

DEVONSHIRE: Greece is a fascinating country, is it not? The people are so eager to oblige foreign citizens. I've heard stories. Some of which defy morality.

BYRON: I don't give a fig for morality. It is only envy thinly disguised.

DEVONSHIRE: I take it then you don't approve of Mister Pitt's committee.

BYRON: The ethics thing? Paying off mothers to turn in their sons for playing with themselves in the dark? It's primitive, barbaric and, as with all things that smack of the Middle Ages, typically English.

DEVONSHIRE: No, I suppose someone whose name has been linked in rumor to stable boys and farmhands would not approve of Mister Pitt's committee.

BYRON: *(Silence; uneasily.)* Again: gossip.

DEVONSHIRE: From very reliable sources.

BYRON: There's no proof to what you say.

DEVONSHIRE: Proof, my Lord Byron, is a thing of the past. I need only speak the word and link your name to it in the morning, you'd be hanging disgraced in the pillory by nightfall. The power of the word is a formidable one. I see why you poets are drawn to it. Today, it is not important that a thing is true, but that it is said to be true. That is the glory of our modern age.

BYRON: There are laws which govern such slander, Your Grace.

DEVONSHIRE: Then pursue them in the courts if you can stand the risk.

BYRON: How dare you? This is an outrage!

DEVONSHIRE: *Au contraire.* This is business. Get me those letters and the Committee on Public Ethics needs never know of your little indiscretions.

BYRON: Why are you doing this? It's absurd! I've never even met Mr. Sheridan!

DEVONSHIRE: You are a writer. You speak his language. I know you will not refuse me.

BYRON: No — I will not involve myself in your seedy little plots! This is no more than bitterness brought on by your disgrace at being passed up for the royal position yourself!

DEVONSHIRE: It is true I have been usurped. The prince forgets that my family, wealth, and title offer more than this common Catholic widow ever could. He also forgets that I am the sort of person who always has the last word. That is what has made me a success. That is why I will not bend. I don't expect a man to understand, but time is a woman's chiefest enemy. Her position in society depends on two things: youth and a good marriage. I have lost the one, I will not lose the other.

BYRON: I will not be the hobbyhorse on which you ride your way to court.

DEVONSHIRE: Oh, but you will.

BYRON: You would drag me through the mud all for a letter?

DEVONSHIRE: My dear Lord Byron, lives have been lost for less. I do so hope you make the right decision. After all, I would very much like to publish — what was it again? *Childe Harold's* something-or-other? I will leave you to consider all your options. *(She turns to go. Stops.)* Oh, and by the by — welcome back to England.

# The Sins of Sor Juana

Karen Zacharias

*Dramatic*

Juana and Silvio (mid-teens)

> *This drama is about Sor Juana Ines de la Cruz, a Roman Catholic nun in seventeenth-century Mexico who was one of the first published poets in the New World. The play imagines the reasons why she became a nun at age seventeen.*

SILVIO: I am surprised and honored that you are suddenly directing a word my way. A week has passed and you have not even met my gaze.

JUANA: Don Silvio, I'm afraid that I owe you an apology.

SILVIO: But if I offended you . . .

JUANA: Señor, I must admit . . . The eve we met, I found your comments disturbing . . . even painful. And I became very angry at you.

SILVIO: For speaking the truth?

JUANA: For giving me hope. *(Pause.)* Your candor, Don Silvio, is the most gracious gift I have ever received. It made me think . . . it made me . . . feel. You appear to have both knowledge and experience.

SILVIO: My family has lived for centuries in the cultured city of Salamanca. The university has been my playground. *(Beat.)* I like to consider myself a professor and tutor in many things.

JUANA: *(Beat.)* And so I approach with a humble question. I have always been alone when . . . But perhaps you . . . Are you able . . . are you willing . . . to possibly teach . . . a woman?

SILVIO: Depends on what the woman would like to learn.

JUANA: Señor, nothing less than the ways of the world.

SILVIO: Really?

JUANA: I am ready for everything. Don't be gentle. *(She hands him some poems.)* Criticize me. Help me improve. Show me the rules of the literary world. Go on . . . read them.

SILVIO: *(Tries to pull himself together.)* Hm. This one is charming although the syntax is a little awkward.

JUANA: Exactly! I thought so as well. And yet . . .

SILVIO: My body answers yours, magnet to metal

But I am not your prize

Boast not of your conquest

Reject me

Slip away from my arms, my breasts

You are still a prisoner

In my poem.

*(Beat.)*

JUANA: Too much?

SILVIO: Sometimes discomfort is completely appropriate.

JUANA: Yes.

SILVIO: "You've undressed my heart, dissolved it

Your hands drowning in its liquid"

*(Beat.)* I would suggest a different word here than *drowning*.

JUANA: But that is the precise word.

SILVIO: Vagueness has its virtues.

JUANA: If I wasn't a lady and you weren't a gentleman, and you were forced to speak your honest mind, with no rules, no avoidance of cruelty. *(Places her hand firmly on his lower arm.)* What would you say of the works before you?

SILVIO: *(Pause; honest).* I would say that they are by no means perfect . . . the meter dances to a strange beat, the rhyme is sometimes forced, and the length on some is . . . But they are eloquent and ferocious . . . betraying a wisdom too ripe for your young years. I would say that whatever you do, you must keep writing. Imperfect poems are the only ones that make a significant impact on the soul. *(Juana kisses the inside of Silvio's hand.)* Juana?

JUANA: Please do not tell the Vicereine of Don Fabio about my behavior. I assure you, I am usually a virtuous, controlled woman.

SILVIO: What a pity.

JUANA: Don Silvio, I have not been able to sleep since the eve we met. I close my eyes and I see you. You are caught between my heart and my voice, trapped inside my eyelids at night. Nothing is right: My blood is thinking and my mind is feeling; I'm going mad . . . and you are making me this way.

SILVIO: But you are to wed another man.

JUANA: Yes! And my reason judged that as the most intelligent, prudent choice to make.

SILVIO: A very sound decision indeed. It ensures your safety and maintenance for the rest of your days. Juana, rest assured that this "impulse" toward me could be nothing more than a whim, a sweet fancy, a craving of some sort . . .

JUANA: Please stop pretending!

SILVIO: Pretending?

JUANA: You are not like the others who pass through these halls. Don't be so polite, so reasonable, so proper. I know what you want.

SILVIO: What do I want?

JUANA: *(Pause).* Everything. You dare hope for everything. It's in your eyes, Don Silvio. *(Beat.)* Why did you come here? My life was decided and clear. I had no pangs. I don't want any man. I don't want any marriage. Ever! And yet, I want you. Why?

SILVIO: I could leave.

JUANA: Yes, but I'm afraid you *(Touches her head.)* will not go away. You spoke words I had thought but had never said out loud.

SILVIO: Words are syllables and air.

JUANA: You said, in your world, a woman would have access to the world. Is that true?

SILVIO: *(Pause.)* I stand by my name.

JUANA: And she would be allowed — no, encouraged — to write, to read, to partake in social intellectual functions? Allowed to shine without compromise or fear? To speak her mind and her heart as loudly as she pleased? And in spite of what others said, you would honor and protect this freedom . . . *her* freedom?

SILVIO: I stand by my name.

JUANA: And you would love her, love her without trying to change her?

SILVIO: I would love *you*, Juana. *(Beat.)* Are these the reasons you seek me out?

JUANA: Honestly, señor, for the first time in my life I am not reaching my decision by reason . . . but trying to reason my impulse. It defies logic. I am going backwards . . . and I know not whether to celebrate freedom or weep defeat.

SILVIO: Can I sway you to rejoice?

JUANA: Only if you tell me that you speak the truth?

SILVIO: *(Pause.)* I stand by my name.

JUANA: I want to believe you.

SILVIO: And I you. How do I know your feelings are true?

JUANA: I assure you, señor, they are.

SILVIO: And if you abandon me like you have Don Fabio?

JUANA: Abandoning you would be like abandoning the best within myself, allowing the rot and moss at the corners of my spirit to move to the center of my being. Don Silvio, abandoning you would be forsaking a gift that God, in all his grace, has given.

SILVIO: *(Pause; Silvio is touched, yet.)* Words. You writers think words are always the answer.

JUANA: What else can I give you, but what I do best?

SILVIO: Dear Juana, a loving, caring, soulful and . . . *tangible* gesture will do more than any poem.

JUANA: *(Pause.)* Monday night, I shall be alone. Meet me then. I will demonstrate the depth of my commitment.

SILVIO: I shall be there. So . . . do you love me, Juana?

JUANA: I think I do. I dream I do. I feel I do.

# The Sins of Sor Juana
## Karen Zacharias

*Dramatic*

Juana and Silvio (mid-teens)

> *This drama is about Sor Juana Ines de la Cruz, a Roman Catholic nun in seventeenth-century Mexico who was one of the first published poets in the New World. The play imagines the reasons why she became a nun at age seventeen.*

SILVIO: *(Pause.)* I was thinking about the poem you gave me . . . It keeps running through my mind.

JUANA: Yes?

SILVIO: I now believe that *drowning* is the precise word. *(Beat.)* This is dangerous.

JUANA: I am a promised woman.

SILVIO: More importantly, you are a woman of promise. And I will not compromise your future.

JUANA: We are that future.

SILVIO: I wish that was true.

JUANA: It is true. Do not leave. *(Pause.)* I have something to give you.

SILVIO: A poem?

JUANA: Something more . . . personal . . . tangible. *(She begins to unhook the front of her dress.)*

SILVIO: Juana . . .

JUANA: Do you want me to stop?

SILVIO: Yes. *(She does. Pause.)* No.

JUANA: Well?

> *(He reaches for her. Juana takes Silvio's hand and places his palm against her stomach and guides it up her body, to her breasts. They embrace. She pulls a cloth from her cleavage and gently pushes him away. She hands him the cloth.)*

JUANA: This is what I wanted to give you.

SILVIO: A cross-stitching?

JUANA: It's one of the most difficult things I've ever done. Did I capture it correctly? Your family crest.

SILVIO: Oh! Now I see it. Of course. The crest.

JUANA: Yes, you see. That's a lion.

SILVIO: Yes.

JUANA: For courage, I suppose.

SILVIO: Yes, and the book for learning. The ship for adventure and . . . what is that?

JUANA: Oh, that. I beg your pardon. That's blood.

SILVIO: Very real.

JUANA: I'm afraid so. *(Shows him her finger.)* I pricked myself.

SILVIO: Badly?

JUANA: It will heal. Pain is part of the process, no?

SILVIO: Unfortunately.

JUANA: And then there's the last design.

SILVIO: The candle.

JUANA: What does the candle stand for?

SILVIO: Many things really. Enlightenment.

JUANA: Interesting . . . especially in light that you are lying to me.

SILVIO: Sorry?

JUANA: Don Silvio, this is not the Tampas family crest. Either you aren't very familiar with your lineage . . . or you are not who you claim to be.

SILVIO: I beg your pardon?

JUANA: Yes, you should. A publisher? From Salamanca? Madrid? Valencia? Where exactly has your family lived for the last century?

SILVIO: Juana, you are confused.

JUANA: Confused, yes. Wrong, no. This crest is a product of imagination. As is, perhaps your name.

SILVIO: You don't know what you are saying.

JUANA: I wanted to make something just for you . . . cross-stitch your family crest. But I did some reading. I discovered there is no you. There is no Tampas family. The contradictions made sense. All I could think is why? Why? Why is this wonderful learned man lying, using a false identity? What profit is there in imitating a nobleman?

SILVIO: I believe this conversation needs to . . .

JUANA: And then suddenly I knew! I knew! I understood!

SILVIO: There is nothing to understand.

JUANA: *(Beat.)* Misbegotten. Illegitimate. Unwanted. *(Beat.)* A bastard.

SILVIO: I have never been so insulted!

JUANA: I find that hard to believe.

SILVIO: I am not a common, wreck of a child like . . . like . . .

JUANA: Like me? *(Pause.)* Marked at conception . . . asking forgiveness for sins that were not ours. Judged by others' low expectations. Guilty until proven innocent. And if I do anything right, I am treated as a carnival curiosity . . . and waved about like a banner. *(Pause.)* That's who I am. Who are you?

SILVIO: Silvio Burgas, bastard son of The Marqués de Gorgóna . . .

JUANA: Why did you not tell me earlier?

SILVIO: And court your disdain?

JUANA: Silvio, you do not understand me.

SILVIO: My mother, my father, and I all cursed the day I was born. Why should you be different?

JUANA: Surely you did not think that . . .

SILVIO: You have discovered my reality. I am but a common man of noble roots. *(Pause. Sincere.)* Juana, I am sorry. *(Begins to exit.)*

JUANA: When I was twelve, I cut my hair, donned boy's clothing and for a brief moment enjoyed a new dimension of possibility.
*(Silvio stops and faces her.)*

JUANA: I was disguised but more myself than I'd ever been. Perhaps masks give the freedom to reveal our deeper truths . . . to reach the point where lies are no longer necessary.

SILVIO: The lies are no longer necessary.

JUANA: And I know all the truths about you?

SILVIO: *(Pause.)* Juana, do not have any illusions. I am a misbegotten . . .

JUANA: Bastard son . . . but hardly common. We must leave while we can.

SILVIO: And go where? I have no name, no wealth, no social gentility . . .

JUANA: Don Silvio, I know the value of gold, the worth of noble birth, the price of power. I have read books on faraway lands, and written poetry from my heart. But, señor, I never dreamed that a man would open so many doors within my soul and that his eyes could become windows to a bright future. Sir, if you search for wealth, seek no further than yourself.

SILVIO: Juana, luxury and comfort are not to be disdained.

JUANA: No. It is pleasure to *live* with them, and a tragedy to live *for* them. I nearly threw away my life for the comfort of living here.

SILVIO: If words were gold . . .

JUANA: They will be. We will earn others' respect, by truly valuing the wealth we possess. The worthiness of our wit, our minds, our words, will open doors. This is a new land; and good things grow from a love that is worthy and true. I promise, as you enrich me, I will enrich you.

SILVIO: *(Pause, removes his chain and places it around Juana's neck.)*
My mother worked her wretched life
She gave me this gold chain
It protected me for twenty years
It is my only worldly gain
All I have and all I am, is yours.

JUANA: And since the soul is the body's life
I will breathe your air, and be your wife.
Let us leave tonight, in secret.
*(They kiss.)*

SILVIO: I'll await you past midnight at the twisted oak that divides the stream. I will not leave without you.

# Splash Hatch on the E Going Down

## Kia Corthron

*Dramatic*

Ollie (thirties) and Thyme (fifteen)

> *Thyme is a black teen and something of a bookworm. Ollie is her father. In this scene, he wakes her up to look at Halley's Comet.*

*Darkness.*

OLLIE: *(Whisper.)* Thyme!

THYME: Huh?

OLLIE: *(Switches light on.)* You 'wake?

THYME: Yeah. *(She is, leaning on her elbow. She is lying on her side of the bed, looking down at the baby next to her in Erry's space. Ollie has binoculars.)*

OLLIE: Wanna see the comet?

THYME: *Here?*

OLLIE: Come on. Your mama listen for the baby. *(Thyme carefully puts the baby in the bassinet, follows Ollie outside. Points.)* There.

THYME: That's a star.

OLLIE: Nope. Comin' home lass night, South Jersey. Pull into this coffee shop, everybody outside lookin' through binoculars. "What?" I say. They point. Amidst the billion billion bright stars, this one stand out for the dullness, faded fuzzy thing. I think, "Oh, guess this be the comet I heard available to the naked eye startin' this week. Big deal."

THYME: That's it? *(He nods.)* Fickle fickle. I've heard it before, every few years, "Comet of the century!" "Brightest sight in the night!" I check the sky latitudes, I set the alarm, four-thirty-three, three-twenty-seven. Promise of something spectacular, untouchable. Nothing. Comet'll change its mind quick, comet'll promise you the fireworks, ambrosia. Then turn of the dime, poof: zero.

OLLIE: This is a zero?

THYME: *(Shrugs.)* Least this time I can say I saw one. Even if it looked nothing like one. The astronomy books.

*(He puts the binoculars against her eyes. She searches. He helps her find it. She gasps. He laughs.)*

THYME: The *tail!*

OLLIE: *That's* the blurry. Couldn't tell in Jersey 'til someone hand me their binocks. *(They gaze at the comet.)* Hadn't been for seein' it in the sticks, identifyin' it, wouldn'ta recognized it in Harlem.

THYME: So close! Don't even need a telescope.

OLLIE: Ain't that a lucky: Harlem only got about five stars, and the comet happen to be one of 'em.

THYME: Dad, makes sense. That comet's ours: our solar system our sun. Lot closer than any of those other stars.

OLLIE: You the math'matician.

THYME: Tail extends several million miles. Twelve hundred and sixty-four, the Chinese recorded it: tail spanning more 'n half the sky! Earth barely a kernel on the comet corn cob.

OLLIE: If that come close to the Earth, whoo! Burn us up!

THYME: People thought that about Halley's, 1910. Daddy, Earth passed right through its tail: No one even noticed. When we've sunk this ship, Earth, that comet'll still be making its regular rounds every hundred years. Or hundred thousand. *(Pause.)* I'm going to the library, get the latest predictions.

OLLIE: You be careful, takin' that baby carriage on the train.

THYME: Believe me, I adhere to all the rules, folding up the stroller, no sticking the stroller in the closing doors. Keep my baby close to my body. *(Taking down the binoculars.)* Just before Erry died, he told me about when he was six and he got on the subway car and his mother following close behind but somehow the subway doors snap shut, she on the outside, and the car flies away, her screaming. Worse, there's some track work ahead so his A's rerouted to the F. But he gets out next stop, tells the token booth woman just like he's been taught to, they call the previous station manager and the happy ending comes fast, Erry in the arms of his hysterical weeping mother. That's a terrifying thing, don't worry: I've no intention of risking that loss.

# Summer Cyclone
## Amy Fox

*Dramatic*

Lucia (thirty-five) and Eugene (ten years younger)

> *In this scene, Lucia is out on a "date" in Coney Island with a doctor at the hospital where she is going for treatment.*

> *Coney Island. Carnival music. Eugene and Lucia enter. Eugene is carrying an orange, stuffed octopus.*

EUGENE: I mean you saw that, right, how many I got.

LUCIA: Which time are you talking about?

EUGENE: What do you mean which time, the last time.

LUCIA: The fifth time.

EUGENE: Yes the fifth time, the time I won.

LUCIA: I would have to say many. It seemed like many prairie dogs were . . . gotten.

EUGENE: Right, many. I think it's groundhogs, I'm not sure but I think. Anyway, many. I got nearly all of them.

LUCIA: It was . . . impressive.

EUGENE: And it was the right choice, wasn't it, the octopus, because that other thing, that purple thing . . .

LUCIA: It was like a sloth.

EUGENE: Yeah, it was, like some kind of sloth. And who needs that, right, a purple sloth thing. I mean definitely the octopus.

LUCIA: No question.

EUGENE: You think it's ridiculous, right, you think I'm . . . young.

LUCIA: You are young.

EUGENE: It's not that big a difference.

LUCIA: How would you know?

EUGENE: I interviewed you.

LUCIA: That's right, you did. Well that takes some of the fun out of small talk, doesn't it.

EUGENE: I'm sorry, we promised we wouldn't mention the study.

LUCIA: Yeah, we did. So how old are you?

EUGENE: Twenty-five.

LUCIA: Almost legal.

EUGENE: For what?

LUCIA: Insight.

EUGENE: That's not exactly fair.

LUCIA: I'm only kidding. I'm sure you understand a great many things.

EUGENE: Some things.

LUCIA: Good. Learn to fake the rest. Good skill for a doctor. You have to explain the world to people.

EUGENE: Not the world . . .

LUCIA: Sometimes. How did you decide, that you wanted to be a doctor.

EUGENE: I hate that question. No matter what you say, it never sounds right . . .

LUCIA: You want to help people.

EUGENE: Something like that. It's the power of knowledge. When things are so . . . cloudy. Because you know things, so you can . . . right, help.

LUCIA: It sounds all right.

EUGENE: My first day of medical school they told us to buy those clicky pens, those pens that change color when you click. They said it would help, to use those for notes, and diagrams. Now it's all you hear, in class, click click click. Sometimes I wonder if anybody's thinking about anything other than switching colors. Click red, click blue. Like kindergarten.

LUCIA: Can't be like that all the time. Cutting up bodies, right, that's not kindergarten.

EUGENE: No.

LUCIA: More like seventh grade, frogs and Styrofoam.

EUGENE: It's pretty different.

LUCIA: I'm sure it is. But look at you, you do look like some kid, you're toting an octopus for God's sake.

EUGENE: I'm not the one who suggested an amusement park.

LUCIA: Fair enough.

EUGENE: And I want that on record, if there's trouble.

LUCIA: You expecting some kind of trouble?

EUGENE: I'm not expecting anything. *(They look at each other, the moment suddenly feels awkward.)* . . . You know I didn't say anything about this, to Dr. Slogan.

LUCIA: I didn't think you would have.

EUGENE: I mean it's none of his business, is it, where you or I go on a Sunday afternoon.

LUCIA: This place is unlike any place in the world. My mom used to take me in the winter, when it was all eerie and deserted.

EUGENE: Yeah, why winter?

LUCIA: I don't know. But I used to get scared, too many ghosts and weirdos running around.

EUGENE: Ghosts?

LUCIA: You know when my mother died, she was cremated and I came here with the ashes to, what's the word, spread . . . scatter . . . release? I can never think of the word.

EUGENE: You did it here?

LUCIA: Yeah, she died in France, and I wasn't there.

EUGENE: My mom died too, when I was sixteen.

LUCIA: Oh — I'm sorry.

EUGENE: Yeah, well, you know . . .

LUCIA: Yeah. Would you . . . want to get some hot dogs? My kitchen at home is full of vegetables and brown rice and extra-firm tofu and I think we should get some hot dogs.

EUGENE: Is it all right?

LUCIA: I don't know, doctor, you tell me.

EUGENE: Sorry, I — hot dogs it is. You like sauerkraut?

LUCIA: Love it.

EUGENE: Just one thing. Take this. *(He holds out the octopus.)*

LUCIA: Oh no you don't.

EUGENE: Take it.

LUCIA: I'm not. I'm sorry.

EUGENE: Take the octopus.

LUCIA: I don't want it.

EUGENE: Neither do I.

LUCIA: You won it. You tried five times.

EUGENE: I was proving myself.

LUCIA: Your ability to conk prairie dogs on the head.

EUGENE: It's groundhogs I'm pretty sure. And I need a backup career.

LUCIA: Yeah, I'm beginning to think you do.

EUGENE: What I don't need is an octopus. *(Eugene pushes the octopus in Lucia's direction. They struggle over it.)*

LUCIA: Fine, I'm taking it and just watch, I'm going to throw in the ocean and something will chew on it and die.

EUGENE: Nothing will touch it. It's the color of macaroni and cheese.

LUCIA: Come on — last chance to save some poor sea creature.

*(She waits to see what Eugene will do. He looks as if he is letting her keep it and then suddenly changes his mind and rushes for it. They struggle some more and find themselves very close together. An awkward moment that could turn into a kiss but doesn't quite. Eugene breaks the moment, turning or stepping back.)*

EUGENE: I think it's about that time.

LUCIA: What time is that?

EUGENE: Cyclone time. What do you say, roller-coaster?

LUCIA: I think I'm already on one.

EUGENE: Let's try that again. Roller-coaster?

LUCIA: Yes. Fuck yes. *(Eugene leads the way.)*

# Virtual Virtue
## Elizabeth Dewberry

*Seriocomic*

Todd and Ella (twenties)

> *Todd and Ella are a couple in their twenties. Todd has been engaging in cybersex, and Ella confronts him about it and tries to persuade him that it's wrong.*

> *Ella: Twenty-something, dressed to impress corporate America. Todd: Twenty-something, wearing jeans and a T-shirt with a cartoon character or something similarly unreal on it. We are in Ella and Todd's apartment. As the light comes up, Ella finishes reading, or rereading, a short stack of pages from a computer printer. She looks impatiently at her watch or a clock. She's mad. Todd enters.*

TODD: Hey, what's up. *(Sensing her mood.)* What?
    *(Ella holds up the papers.)*
TODD: *(Feigning innocence.)* What?
ELLA: *(Deadpan, reading from the papers.)* Big'n'hard —
    *(She looks up at him.)* I presume that's you?
TODD: Not at the moment.
ELLA: *(Rolling her eyes, then reading again, alternating between imitations of Angelbaby and Todd.)* Big'n'hard, I dreamed about you last night . . . What'd you dream, Angelbaby? . . . We were on the beach and I was wearing this little sarong skirt with no panties and you untied —
TODD: Oh good grief.
ELLA: Sweetie, "good grief" is what Charlie Brown says when Lucy yanks his football out from under him.
TODD: It's an expression.
    *(He shrugs: What's the big deal?)*

ELLA: Right. As in, "My boyfriend, Big'n'hard, is cheating on me with some computer bimbo named Angelbaby. Oh good grief!"

TODD: *(Incredulous.)* I'm not cheating on you. That's not who I am.

ELLA: I'm your girlfriend. I'm not Angelbaby. You're having cybersex with Angelbaby. Ergo, you're cheating on me.

TODD: Cybersex is not sex.

ELLA: Well, in the words of Bill Clinton, I guess that depends on what your definition of "is" is.

TODD: Don't do this, Ella.

ELLA: Don't tell me what to do.

TODD: I'm asking you not to turn self-righteous and sarcastic on me. Honey, she doesn't even know my name. We're not real to each other. For all I know, she's a three-hundred-pound man.

ELLA: *(Sarcastically.)* Oh! I see! And I mean this nonsarcastically: What you're saying is that not knowing who she is makes having sex with her OK!

TODD: That is not what I said.

ELLA: You know what bothers me the most? Aside from the fact that you're having this little affair at all —

TODD: Would you stop acting like you don't even know me? I am not a lying cheat.

ELLA: The detail that really gets to me? She can't spell! You have this . . . whatever-you-want-to-call-it . . . that only exists in writing, and she spells it *fetish* with two T's. It's just . . . ick. What do you see in this person?

TODD: Nothing. Come on, you're the only one whose spelling *means* anything to me. I don't even notice the other woman's spelling.

ELLA: You really do think this is funny, don't you? *(She's more hurt than mad now, and he puts his arm around her to comfort her.)*

TODD: Hey, I'm sorry. But Angelbaby is . . . she's like a character in a novel. I don't get jealous when you read romance novels.

ELLA: I don't read romance novels. But if I did, I wouldn't expect my "characters" to dream about me undressing them, and I wouldn't —

TODD: OK, it's more like . . . an interactive novel. I'm a fictional character too.

ELLA: I wouldn't come up with a stupid name for myself like . . . Wet'n'Juicy —

TODD: Not for several months.

ELLA: And I wouldn't promise to make my "characters" dreams come true.

TODD: It's a game.

ELLA: And you and Angelbaby are merely players in it!

TODD: Right!

ELLA: Todd, at the risk of sounding like a responsible adult, it's *wrong.*

TODD: Unlike being angry, resentful, smug, and self-pitying, not to mention no fun anymore?

ELLA: That's what you see in her?

*(Todd gestures: What?)*

ELLA: She doesn't ask you for a commitment, doesn't tell you to put the toilet seat down, doesn't need you to deal with her feelings when you hurt her?

TODD: I told you. All I see in her is that she's not real.

*(Beat.)*

ELLA: Well, I can't compete with that.

TODD: Why would you want to?

ELLA: Todd, how could you not know why I wouldn't want to, unless you *do* know, and you want me to want to?

TODD: What?

ELLA: I don't want to compete with a lover who's not real because I am, moods and zits and all, and my feelings are real. I love you. But you also irritate the hell out of me, and I can't just turn you off, and I can't stand it when I feel you're turning *me* off. *(Beat. She grabs her purse, goes to the door.)* I'm going for a walk.

TODD: Don't you dare walk out that door.

ELLA: Don't you dare me not to.

TODD: You're not playing fair.

ELLA: I'm not playing.

TODD: Look, I may not be the world's easiest person to live with, but neither are you. So I went on the Internet to have a little fun. But I'm still here.

*(She shakes her head: That's not enough. She puts her hand on the doorknob and waits with her back to him for him to stop her.)*

TODD: I could have done this with a real woman, but I didn't. Because of you. *(Pause.)*

ELLA: *(Without looking at him.)* Then you're a fool.

*(She exits. He watches the door close behind her as he flips on the computer. It hums its start-up refrain as he sits down in front of it. He smiles and relaxes, turns off the lights, and lets the world disappear when he hears . . . )*

COMPUTER'S HUMANOID FEMALE VOICE: Welcome. You've got mail.

TODD: *(Typing as he talks.)* Hi Angelbaby. It's me, uh, Big'n'hard. My real . . .

# Scenes for Women

# Be Aggressive
## Annie Weissman

*Seriocomic*

Laura and Leslie (teens)

> *Laura and Leslie are two teenaged girls on the cheerleading team. They have borrowed Mom's car and ATM card and are on a cross-country quest to find, and enroll in, a mysterious school for cheerleaders where they can learn some totally awesome routines.*
>
> *Lights up. Loud, loud music. Laura and Leslie in the car. Leslie drives. They both have harnesses around their waists into which are fitted sixty-four-ounce Diet Cokes. The music stops. Long pause. Laura and Leslie breathe, very full of air and liquid.*

LAURA: Did you know that seahorses are the only animal species in the oceanic kingdom or otherwise, in which the male carries the babies? *(Beat.)* And the males are nesters, too. They can stay on one blade of sea grass for like, three whole years. Hence, their vulnerability. *(Pause.)*

LESLIE: You're not gonna be one of those people who fills the quiet spaces with like, metaphors, are you?

LAURA: God! I was just . . . thinking.

*(They both slurp their drinks, then sputter to a stop. Empty. Pause.)*

LESLIE: So, what else?

LAURA: *(Pouting.)* What?

LESLIE: About the seahorses.

LAURA: Well, Chinese herbalists use their desiccated and pulverized corpses to heal many injuries and ailments. Like gout, rheumatism . . .

LESLIE: What are those?

LAURA: Diseases.

LESLIE: Oh. *(Long pause.)* What else?

LAURA: That's all I remember. *(Beat.)*

LESLIE: Where are we?

LAURA: We're getting closer.

LESLIE: How much longer?

LAURA: *(Refers to the map.)* Like, eight inches.

LESLIE: Good. We'll be there soon.

LAURA: But in the last eight hours we went like, half an inch.

LESLIE: Laura, I'm the one who remembered to steal my mom's triple A card, I'm the one who got the maps with it, I'm the one who split the line into three's and picked the stop points. So, if you have a better plan than mine for getting us there then say so. 'K?

LAURA: Well, I got the ATM card.

LESLIE: I know, and I'm grateful for that. That was a good call on your part. *(Beat.)* What's the code? I need greens bad. Let's stop and get cash and get salads.

LAURA: Um.

LESLIE: Oh my God.

LAURA: No, I know it. I know it.

LESLIE: You don't know the fucking code.

LAURA: No, no. I knew it. I swear. Fuck.

LESLIE: We were relying on that card. I got the car, you got the cash. What the hell are we gonna do?

LAURA: I know it, I swear. Just be quiet and I'll think of it. *(Beat.)* It's my sister's middle name, no that's our security system disarmer. Shit. I know it stands for something. It's some important thing in our lives. Fuck! What is it?

LESLIE: This is just great. Great! The one thing I ask you to take care of, and you don't have the courtesy to follow through. You are totally careless, you know that? *(Beat. Stunned.)* That was my mother!

LAURA: I'm sorry, it's just that somehow it's out of my head, out here. I look out and see all these, like, the lands, and somehow, that code, just, isn't there anymore.

LESLIE: You didn't get any extra cash! No spending money?

LAURA: I just got the tuition. Eight hundreds, two fifties, and five twenties.

LESLIE: You didn't even get any ones?

LAURA: I didn't think about it.

LESLIE: What about tipping? Huh? How are we gonna tip?

LAURA: I don't think you tip at like, motels.

LESLIE: We're gonna have to live off the Mobil card.

LAURA: You got the Mobil card?

LESLIE: Yes, of course I got the Mobil card. I said I was going to, and I did. That's how I work. Great. We're going to have to eat off the gas station now. This is just great. For three days. What are we gonna eat? Microwave mini-burgers? Corn dogs?

LAURA: They have yogurts there. Sometimes.

LESLIE: Yeah, like whole fat banana flavor.

LAURA: Well they have those turkey things don't they, those triangle sandwiches?

LESLIE: You're kidding, right? Those cat-food-quality cold cuts, on Wonder bread, with iceberg, and mayonnaise? *(Beat.)* Why don't we just get a brick of pork lard and a couple of soup spoons?

LAURA: Well maybe we could separate the turkey, that's all, and wipe off the mayo. And just eat the slices. *(Beat.)* 'K?

LESLIE: *(Beat.)* OK.

*(Long pause. They have reached an open place. There are fields.)*

LAURA: What do you think they're growing?

LESLIE: I don't know. Corn. Cotton. Hay. Something.

LAURA: Hay?

LESLIE: I don't know.

LAURA: When do they pick, you think?

LESLIE: I don't know.

LAURA: How many corns on a plant? Like three? Or like twenty? Do they rip 'em out and redo 'em every year, or do the corns just wait under the weather and come back in the sun?

LESLIE: I don't know. *(Pause.)*

LAURA: How many jog bras did you bring?

LESLIE: Eight. You?

LAURA: Eight. How many books?

LESLIE: None. You?

LAURA: One.

LESLIE: What?

LAURA: *Roots.*

LESLIE: *Roots?*

LAURA: It's African-American Week in World Lit. *(Beat.)* Have you ever tried the corn wrap?

LESLIE: Already talked about that!

LAURA: Who's your favorite trainer at Vista del Body and Soul?

LESLIE: Already talked about that, too!

LAURA: 'K. *(Silence. More fields.)* Why don't we open the windows?

LESLIE: I have the AC on.

LAURA: Yeah, but why don't we try it for a bit. Let something in. *(Leslie opens the windows. Long silence. Leslie closes the windows.)*

LESLIE: That's enough.

LAURA: What did your dad do?

LESLIE: A spokesmodel. She sold resistance training rubber bands gym to gym. He moved away with her. He hasn't communicated with me in a calendar year. *(Long pause.)*

LAURA: Elastercizers?

LESLIE: Yeah, those.

LAURA: Nobody uses those anymore. Now that there's the new latex bands.

LESLIE: I know. They're twice as supple without compromising any of the strength. *(Beat.)* I don't know what he does now. *(Pause.)* Are we in Utah, yet?

LAURA: I haven't seen a sign.

LESLIE: My neck hurts.

LAURA: Well, pull over. It should be my turn to drive by now.

LESLIE: I'm not pulling over until we get to Utah.

LAURA: There should be an automatic neck adjustment. Our Lexus has a weight-sensitive neck support.

LESLIE: So does Tracy's mom's Lexus. So does Stacie's mom's Lexus. But my mom has to get the stripped model, of course! Everybody else gets the turkey, and my mom gets the carcass! *(Beat.)*

LAURA: Is Utah . . . on the way to the South?

LESLIE: Look, I've skied there. Do you have a plan?

LAURA: No.

LESLIE: *(Final.)* Then, Utah.

LAURA: 'K. *(Lights shift.)*

# Hard Feelings

## Neena Beber

*Comic*

Selma and Finola (twenties to thirties)

>*Selma and Finola are two roommates/girlfriends. Finola is leaving, much to Selma's dismay.*

>*Selma's place. Finola has some suitcases packed and ready to go. She is adding a few things to her bags when Selma enters.*

SELMA: What are you doing?

FINOLA: I'm leaving you, Selma. I've met somebody else. Please don't make a big deal of it or think you're more hurt than you are. We both know this relationship ended long ago. I haven't been emotionally available to you for many months now, as I'm sure you've noticed, and if you haven't you should have which is another sign of how far apart we've grown.

*(Selma starts to whimper.)*

FINOLA: Please don't cry. The time will come when you will thank me for recognizing the need for closure on this particular chapter in both our lives. Good-bye, Selma. If you can't find a new roommate within the month, for the next two weeks I've decided to pay half of my third, i.e. one-eighth of the rent.

SELMA: A fourth, actually —

FINOLA: All right, you do the math. The point is our journey is over.

*(Selma sits, still stunned.)*

FINOLA: You're going to see what a wonderful thing this will be for you. I bought you a present. *(Handing over a package.)* Just my way of saying, "Thank you, time well spent, now let's give each other room to evolve."

*(Selma begins crying.)*

FINOLA: Come, Selma, please don't. If you want to get into it, I don't even believe you're gay. Just because you hate men doesn't make you a lesbian. Although I admit that hating men to the extent that you do and being a heterosexual woman does put you in a bit of a pickle. That's a tough one indeed. Open my prezy, Selma, I think you'll like it.

SELMA: Don't leave me. Please don't leave me.

FINOLA: All right, I'll open it for you. *(Finola opens the box: fuzzy green slippers with rabbit ears.)* Fuzzy slippers, see? Aren't they precious? They're bunnies, green bunnies, isn't that absolutely precious? I almost got you a pair of well-worn comfy P.J.'s but when I saw they had these dear old bunnies, I couldn't resist.

SELMA: They're used?

FINOLA: Vintage. Try them on, Selma.

SELMA: Plus I didn't get into Dr. Disposio's class.

FINOLA: That writing teacher rejected you after all?

SELMA: He gave me a book instead.

FINOLA: See there? It's a prezy day.

SELMA: I had to pay for it. Twenty-five bucks. It doesn't even have a cover yet.

FINOLA: Put on the slippers and I'll make you a cup of tea. In the morning you'll have a clear head about this, a fresh perspective, plus you'll have your fuzzy slippers. Trust me?

SELMA: Don't do this . . . please don't do this.

*(Selma begins to sob rather loudly.)*

FINOLA: Your granny's sleeping, Selma. You mustn't not control yourself. You really mustn't not.

SELMA: *(Shouting through sobs.)* I hate double negatives.

FINOLA: It may be my issue, but you know how uncomfortable I am with tears.

SELMA: *(Still shouting and sobbing.)* You're a grief counselor.

FINOLA: I really didn't want it to be this way. Good-bye, Selma, I've posted my forwarding number on the refrigerator. *(Opening her arms for a hug.)* No hard feelings?

SELMA: *(Refusing her.)* All feelings are hard.

FINOLA: I'm offering you closure, Selma. Say "Good-bye, Finola Cornflakes, thank you for a wonderful journey" or someday, I guarantee you'll wish you had.

*(Nothing. Finola shrugs and goes.)*

SELMA: *(Calling after.)* Your name — is really stupid — you have a really stupid name.

# Hold Please
## Annie Weissman

*Comic*

Jessica and Erika (twenties)

*Jessica and Erika are coworkers in an office. Erika reveals that she is pregnant by a male coworker boss type.*

*The office. Jessica reads to Erika from Diana's memoir.*

JESSICA: "While it may be a useful exercise to question such things as organized religion, patriarchy, and antibiotics, in the end, we should acknowledge that Americans in the twenty-first century are, in the immortal words of Tina Turner, 'Simply the Best!' We have freedom, we have abundance, and most important of all —" and this is in bold faced caps cuz it's also the title of her book — "WE CAN DO WAY MORE THAN THEY TELL US WE CAN!"

ERIKA: Where is she?

JESSICA: Lunch. She'll be back to give us the results.

ERIKA: When?

JESSICA: In an hour.

ERIKA: Did she say you could read that?

JESSICA: She ASKED me to. This will be a blockbuster book. It's gonna do Dr. Laura numbers. It will get called "a stunning debut" by *Entertainment Weekly.* Listen to her political views, "Bill Clinton appointed more fat old women to more posts formerly held by fat old men than any president before him. He quietly altered the dynamics of gender in government, FOREVER. So he got serviced on the side. Got his floor mopped. His engine coolant drained. Big deal! Most wives would be relieved to be relieved of the duty! It certainly didn't make him any less of a leader, role model, or man!" Can you BELIEVE her?

ERIKA: Who do you think won the contest?

JESSICA: It's not a contest, it's an efficiency project.

ERIKA: It's a contest. And one of us is going to win.

JESSICA: Know where I heard she gets her edge? Pharmaceutical testosterone! Supposedly she was born with both. And the people who
raised her, they waited what today would be considered far too long
to decide which end of the rope she was to tug on. So now she reg-
ulates her own testosterone levels! I'm gonna try it!

ERIKA: Who told you that?

JESSICA: My phone friend at TTD. She hears everything.

ERIKA: Testosterone?

JESSICA: I believe it! Jonathan's uncle is a former physician's assistant and
he still has prescription pads. Wanna try it?

ERIKA: You don't know what that stuff could do to you!

JESSICA: Oh Nancy, go tell it to Ronnie. You're such a throwback sometimes. Such a prude!

ERIKA: I'm pregnant.

*(Beat.)*

JESSICA: You are not!

ERIKA: I am.

JESSICA: You sure?

ERIKA: Yep.

JESSICA: Gyno?

ERIKA: Over-the-counter.

JESSICA: First Response?

ERIKA: EPT.

JESSICA: When?

ERIKA: Last night.

JESSICA: How far?

*(Pause.)*

ERIKA: Remember when I had those marks on my leg? Those diamond-
shaped imprints? Well remember how we ordered the floor mats for
the exec suites and we opted for the premium plexiglass for added
swivel chair mobility? And they all have that diamond-shaped pat-
tern pressed deep into their surface.

*(Beat.)*

JESSICA: Xavier?

ERIKA: No! Solomon.

JESSICA: Eww! Solomon? You fell victim to an exploitation of assymetry and a flagrant abuse of power?

ERIKA: No! I didn't fall victim to anything! We were attracted to each other, and we became lovers! It's a relationship!

JESSICA: Bullshit!

ERIKA: I'm his mistress!

JESSICA: You're his home-wrecking secretary!

ERIKA: You don't know what I am! You don't know what goes on between us!

JESSICA: Yeah, and neither does his WIFE! And FAMILY!

ERIKA: His wife is nuts, OK? You should SEE the meds he has to get for her, the cocktails of antidepressants and antipsychotics. She drives him insane! And this is a man who is already under a lot of pressure! And often in a great deal of pain! I massage his lower back and that is where he stores a lot of painful memories. He sometimes shares them with me.

*(Beat. Jessica makes a disapproving sound.)*

ERIKA: He shares A LOT with me. You don't know. And sexually, he's a completely different person from the one you see in the well-cut suit, bossing people around. He's actually really shy. It's so cute. I'm telling you, the way he touches me — it's soft, and gentle. Even when we're only on the plexiglass floor mat. *(Beat.)* I know it's not emotional. I'm not a fucking IDIOT. I just happen to have very soft skin. I've been ruthlessly exfoliating since my mother gave me my first loofah, at age eight. I know I'm just something that feels good to touch. But still, you should see how he gets with me. He's like a great big little boy.

*(Pause.)*

JESSICA: I remember the first time I saw Jonathan. He was standing outside, in the part of the parking lot where the smokers go smoke. He had one green Puma sneaker propped up against the wall and he was leaning back all East of Eden-ish. He was doing this thing with his

Zippo lighter. He was turning it over and over and over in his hands. Stroking its surface. Here was this scruffy-looking guy, I mean greasy khaki pants and this torn-up denim jacket and his hair was stiff with filth and there he was just appreciating the smoothness of the thing in his hands. Without having to TALK about it, you know? Without having to turn to some friend of his and go, "Hey look what I'm doing" the way, you know, a girl would. Guys don't seem to have to TALK about things in order to feel them. They can feel things fine on their own. In silence. *(Beat.)* You know what I mean?

ERIKA: Yes.

JESSICA: You know what I'm talking about, right?

ERIKA: I do. *(Beat.)* Solomon's car is huge and powerful, but it has this really quiet engine. Sometimes, afterwards, when he's driving me home, this phrase comes in to my head, over and over again — "full-size luxury sedan."

*(Beat.)*

JESSICA: So Xavier never . . .

ERIKA: No.

JESSICA: So we just —

ERIKA: Yes.

JESSICA: And his wife has —

ERIKA: Terminal.

JESSICA: Man! *(Beat.)* What are you gonna do?

ERIKA: I'm probably gonna leave and go get a job with a little more flexibility, so I can grow and have more me-time. One of those Web site jobs, or something.

JESSICA: Those jobs are already over!

ERIKA: Well you were thinking about it.

JESSICA: Not any more! Just from a professional point of view I'd say that judging from the new pace of things around here a pregnancy would really slow you down. It's not some Scarlet Letter moral issue, it's just that you couldn't keep up if you were pregnant . . . *(Beat.)* What did Solomon say? You're not stupid enough to think he's gonna leave his wife for you, are you? You don't think you have a future with him, do you? *(Beat.)* Diana's gonna be back from lunch any minute you know. She's asked me to deliver the results to all of us in the break room. I have a meeting with her when she gets back, so maybe you should go cover the phones now.

ERIKA: This isn't the nineties!

JESSICA: What's that supposed to mean?

ERIKA: I don't know. That I have options!

JESSICA: Right. Why don't you go cover the phones, OK? And get off your feet? We have a very important meeting in a few minutes.

ERIKA: I have choices.

JESSICA: Just as an FYI, you can see right through your shirt to your nipples. Diana told me to tell you that. If you're going to continue on the work track, you might want to invest in a decent blazer or at least a couple of opaque camisoles.

ERIKA: So you and your GIRLFRIEND sit around and talk about my nipples? Why don't you just go ahead and start a softball league?

JESSICA: You just don't have the maturity to understand a female model of mentorship.

ERIKA: I understand that you're jealous of me.

JESSICA: Yes, if only I could be a twenty-five-year-old pregnant semipermanent secretary with flagrantly visible nipples!

ERIKA: You're semipermanent too!

JESSICA: I'm entry level! I'm on my way up! *(Beat.)* You know, you need to go cover the phones. I have information to receive.

# Late Night in the Womens' Restroom in the Jungle Bar

David Riedy

*Comic*

Karen and Haley (twenties to thirties)

> *Haley has fled her ostensibly happy home and come to a local bar in search of Karen, a friend who can take her in, at least for the night.*

> *The bathroom of a dive bar in Upper West Side Manhattan, 11:00 PM. The door swings open, banging into the back wall, letting in a stale blast of nondescript loud pop music with entirely too much bass. The music brings Haley in with it. She is carrying a heavy suitcase in one hand and pulling Karen through the door with the other.*

KAREN: — but you don't understand — I was talking to Jerry!

HALEY: I know. I'm sorry —

KAREN: I can't leave him out there alone.

HALEY: I really need to talk to you.

KAREN: Could we talk tomorrow?

HALEY: It's important.

KAREN: Yeah but —

HALEY: It'll just take a minute, I promise.

KAREN: OK. But just a minute. *(Sees suitcase.)* Oh. You have a suitcase. How come you have a suitcase?

HALEY: I left Ben.

KAREN: You did?!?

HALEY: Yes.

KAREN: Wow. Who's Ben?

HALEY: My husband.

KAREN: Oh. Ohmygod! You left your — I mean you *just* left your — tonight?

HALEY: Yes!

KAREN: And you came to see me?

HALEY: You invited me.

KAREN: But you came.

HALEY: Is that OK?

KAREN: Yes — that's — but *tonight!* I'm sorry.

HALEY: *(Confused.)* What?

KAREN: Are you OK?

HALEY: No.

KAREN: I should do something for you. You want a drink?

HALEY: No.

KAREN: OK. You want a hug?

HALEY: No. Thanks.

KAREN: OK. *(Beat.)* I really have to go back out —

HALEY: Can I stay with you tonight?

KAREN: Oh. Um.

HALEY: Your roommate's still in Spain, right?

KAREN: Yeah, but —

HALEY: It's just for tonight. You're the only person I can go to.

KAREN: But, I thought you didn't like me. You never have lunch with me when I ask.

HALEY: Of course I like you.

KAREN: You didn't come to my birthday party.

HALEY: I know, I'm sorry. I think Ben had a thing —

KAREN: Sure. It's just — this may sound kind of silly — and I know you're going through all this emotional turmoil and all — but I've always really liked you and I've always thought we could be really good friends — and so it means a lot to me that you came to me, you know, when you were upset.

HALEY: Well, sure.

KAREN: So, I *want* to say yes, but — if I say no does that make me a bad person?

HALEY: I've been walking for hours. I just need a place to sleep.

KAREN: I don't want to be selfish, but my therapist says it's OK for me to stick up for myself —

HALEY: I'm sorry I never go out to lunch with you. I like to eat alone —

KAREN: You went out with Mary from Mr. Helprin's office.

HALEY: She paid.

KAREN: I'd pay.

HALEY: We'll have lunch on Monday, I promise.

KAREN: OK! But — it's not about that.

HALEY: What is it?

KAREN: It's Jerry.

HALEY: Who's Jerry?

*(Karen starts to put more makeup on.)*

KAREN: I was talking to him when you came in —

HALEY: Right — and . . . ?

KAREN: Well, I met him last week and we really hit it off. He bought me like four or five drinks and we talked and talked and he asked me if I would go home with him, but I wasn't comfortable with that because I hardly knew him and he said he could respect that (!) and that he'd meet me here again, tonight, to try to convince me because he said he Really Likes Me — and he's out there right now! — and so, Julia's in Spain you know, and I usually sleep on the couch — it folds into a bed — but I pay less rent than Julia so it's OK — and I thought I could take Jerry — back to my place and we could sleep in Julia's room and it would be OK because I'd feel better being in my own apartment. But I don't want him to know where I live, so I'll tell him it's Julia's apartment and that I'm taking care of her cat while she's in Spain. She doesn't have a cat, but I'll tell him it's hiding because it's scared.

*(Beat. Haley stares at Karen for an uncomprehending moment.)*

HALEY: *(Moaning in frustration:)* Oh Gooooooooooooood . . . !

KAREN: I'm really sorry.

HALEY: I don't have any place to go!

KAREN: What about your parents?

HALEY: They live in Arizona.

KAREN: Oh. Well, don't you have any other friends . . .?

HALEY: They're all Ben's friends. They'd tell him I was there.

KAREN: And you don't want him to know — ?

HALEY: No!

KAREN: What about Mary?

HALEY: I hate Mary. I only went to lunch with her because she's good friends with Bill Peterman who was looking for a new assistant.

KAREN: Oh. Did you get the job?

HALEY: No. Karen — please, you can bring Jerry home. He'll never know I'm there. I'll sleep in the bathtub.

KAREN: But there's only one bathroom —

HALEY: I'll sleep in the *closet.*

KAREN: I want to help. I do! But — I don't know. I wish Bridget was here.

HALEY: Bridget?

KAREN: She's kind of like my coach. You know her — she just started two weeks ago —

HALEY: The one with the body and the tight bright suits?

KAREN: She's real nice. She introduced me to Jerry. She's helping me with — I've been really nervous because I haven't been with a man in three years. Since Ronnie left.

HALEY: Who's Ronnie?

KAREN: This guy that I was in love with for five years and who promised he was going to marry me and then dumped me for my former best friend. I'm over him now, though.

HALEY: I know I'm asking a lot — but I don't have any other choice. I left my purse at home. I don't have any money.

KAREN: Neither do I.

HALEY: I'm not asking for money —

KAREN: I think he might be another Ronnie.

HALEY: Who?

KAREN: Jerry!

HALEY: WELL HE'S NOT! HE'S NOT ANOTHER RONNIE! YOU ONLY GET ONE RONNIE! YOU ONLY GET *ONE!* And *yes,* it makes you a horrible person and a bad friend and a selfish bitch! You're always nice to me at work, flipping your hair, saying "hi!" and asking me to lunch but when I really need your help you'd rather have sex with some stranger, than — !

*(Beat. Haley gets control of herself.)*

I'm sorry. I hardly know you.

KAREN: No. It's OK. You're kind of right.

HALEY: I'm the one who's being a bad person.

KAREN: No. You're upset. You just left your husband. That's probably pretty upsetting. I wouldn't know. But it probably is.

HALEY: You've always been so sweet to me and I thought I could — When I left the apartment I just started walking. I walked for almost two hours, wandering up and down the streets with my stupid suitcase. I went into a Barnes and Noble and sat down in the children's section, and I started reading *Little House on the Prairie.*

KAREN: I love that book! I have —

HALEY: — that picture of Laura on the wall by your desk, right! And you'd asked me if I wanted to have a drink with you tonight and — it was like I was supposed to ask you for help. And I'm exhausted and miserable and I just need a place to stay for one night — until I can get into the apartment while he's at work. *(Beat.)* Please, Karen.

KAREN: I . . . OK.

# Quake
## Melanie Marnich

*Comic*

Lucy (twenties to thirties) and That Woman (a little older)

> *This very inventive comedy is about a woman's search for Mr. Right. Jux-*
> *taposed with various scenes between Lucy and various "unsuitable" men*
> *are scenes with That Woman, a serial killer on the lam. In this scene,*
> *Lucy finally meets That Woman who, she finds, has a new career — as*
> *a housewife!*

> *It's a deep blue night in San Francisco. Lucy finds her way to a park*
> *bench. She notices That Woman sitting next to her, knitting.*

LUCY: It's you.

THAT WOMAN: Get lost.

LUCY: I know you.

THAT WOMAN: No you don't.

LUCY: Yes I do.

THAT WOMAN: No you don't.

LUCY: We met. A long time ago. In a different place.

THAT WOMAN: No we didn't.

LUCY: I know you.

THAT WOMAN: No you don't.

LUCY: I recognize you.

THAT WOMAN: Impossible. I've had complete reconstructive surgery.

LUCY: You're That Woman.

THAT WOMAN: My name is Peggy Papsi. I'm married to an insurance guy.
    I have two kids and a dog. I'm suburban. I'm fine. I'm normal. I'm
    on the PTA. I do bake sales. So don't fuck with me. Fuck off. You
    don't fucking know me. You never fucking saw me. And if you fuck-

ing keep insisting, I'll fuck with you. I'm going to knit now. I came
here to relax. My husband's on the phone and the kids are on Ri-
talin. Dropped a stitch. Goddammit.

LUCY: You seem tense.

THAT WOMAN: I'm fine. Fuck off.

LUCY: You.

THAT WOMAN: Me what?

LUCY: You . . . you know.

THAT WOMAN: Me fuck off?

LUCY: Yeah. How could you go get married and all that?

THAT WOMAN: You're pushing my buttons, Bambi.

LUCY: But you're my hero, my idol. You never settled and you never slowed
down. I love that. You swagger. Inside. I love that. You kept moving
and you weren't afraid. I love that. You're everything I'm not. I love
that. You got under my skin, on my mind, in my sleep. And I kept
moving like you. Place to place, like you. Looking for the love of
my life. And you said don't stop.

THAT WOMAN: I never said that. Prove I said that. I never said that.

LUCY: Liar. So I didn't. I didn't stop. And now look at me. Look at you.

THAT WOMAN: You got it all wrong. Everyone had it wrong. All I wanted
to do was stop. But not here. I was going to build rockets, you know.
I wanted to be the star of stellar phenomena, but I was a problem
because I was a scientist who believed in magic.

 I was furious. Furious was my destiny. The day I taught myself
to make a fist, they told me to sip my tea. When I beat my chest,
they told me to cross my legs. Fuck. That.

 Whoever the hell you are, know this. I am brilliant. And that
is pure energy. Energy doesn't disappear. Can't disappear. No matter what the courts say. No matter what the doctors say. It's nature,
it's science, it's out of my hands.

 Then one day I was looking at the sky and Polaris said hello.
Orion said it's nice up here. Scorpio said we saved a place for you.
And I knew where I needed to be. Past the fifth sky is seventh heaven.
Is that Ursa Major or Ursa Minor?

LUCY: It's the Golden Gate, I think.

THAT WOMAN: I'm a little rusty.

LUCY: I needed to find you. I need to know. What did it take to stop you? A car chase? A fight? A knife? A bullet? Someone so magnificent?

THAT WOMAN: Thought it would take a rocket but it only took a rock, someone who'd hold my hand when we crossed the street.

LUCY: That's all?

THAT WOMAN: No.

LUCY: Is there such a thing as a perfect love?

THAT WOMAN: You're asking *me*?

LUCY: Yeah.

*(That Woman thinks. Hard.)*

THAT WOMAN: Absolutely.

*(Lucy sighs. Relief.)*

THAT WOMAN: Just depends on how many flaws you're willing to put up with.

*(Lucy sighs.)*

THAT WOMAN: Before I was furious, I was afraid. Like an animal, like a baby. That feeling. I hated it. Sometimes I miss it. *(She knits a few stitches.)* The earth spins a little slower now. The riot's gone.

It's almost quiet. But not quite. Some days when I'm driving I look in the mirror and everything I've done is right behind me, screaming and gaining. That's what it's like on a bad day. But I have good days, too. My best days are nights when I sit on my porch and look at the sky. The people I love are sleeping inside my house. I guard them and look at the stars.

I know I can still throw sparks. Still launch myself if I have to. Live up there if I want. But not now. I'm gonna stay here for a while. *(Noticing Lucy staring at her.)* What are you looking at? Quit staring at me. Freak.

LUCY: You are just so different.

THAT WOMAN: What did you expect?

LUCY: Something else.

THAT WOMAN: Disappointed?

LUCY: Maybe. A little.

THAT WOMAN: Hey. Look. There. It's the Big Dipper.

LUCY: It's the lights from Alcatraz.

THAT WOMAN: Oh. Yeah. Guess it is.

    *(They sit.)*

THAT WOMAN: I'm not what you expected. I'm not what *I* expected.

    *(That Woman exits. Lucy is alone.)*

LUCY: I know.

# Wonderful World
Richard Dresser

*Comic*

Patty and Jennifer (thirties to forties)

> *In this scene, Patty and Jennifer are negotiating going out to lunch and their relationship.*

> *Lights up on an office area. Two chairs: one straight and severe, the other large and soft. Jennifer is in the soft chair, sunk down deep into it. She's been waiting a long time. Patty appears, dressed for business. Jennifer doesn't see her.*

PATTY: Jennifer? There you are!

JENNIFER: Patty! Hi. I think I fell asleep.

> *(Jennifer struggles out of the chair, dazed. She starts to hug Patty, who stops her with a firm handshake.)*

JENNIFER: *(Continuing.)* I often fall asleep when I'm nervous. Once I heard a burglar in the house and I was going to call 911 and my heart was pounding in terror and then I woke up and it was morning.

PATTY: So there was really nothing to worry about.

JENNIFER: Except everything that I owned was gone. Shoes, pills, thongs, dolls.

PATTY: Are you nervous now?

JENNIFER: Not now. Not really. No.

PATTY: I'm not late, am I?

JENNIFER: No. Well, maybe a teensy little bit . . .

PATTY: We said twelve-thirty, right?

JENNIFER: Actually, not that it matters, we said twelve, so I got here fifteen minutes early but it's really OK.

PATTY: Did you tell anyone you were here?

JENNIFER: No. Not yet. I thought you were busy.

PATTY: I am. I had to let my assistant go this morning.

JENNIFER: Oh, dear. That must be very hard.

PATTY: Yes, the paperwork is endless.

JENNIFER: I can imagine. *(Beat.)* What did he or she do?

PATTY: Do?

JENNIFER: To get let go.

PATTY: Is this just a polite question or do you really want to know?

JENNIFER: Well, I hope it's polite . . . but I really want to know.

PATTY: Very well, I had to let my assistant go because he or she wasted my time.

JENNIFER: Oh, dear! That's awful. Well. Shall we . . . go?

PATTY: Where?

JENNIFER: I made a reservation at Connolly's. I'm starved and I only get an hour. Actually now it's half an hour.

PATTY: Was this for lunch?

JENNIFER: Yes. I'm taking you out to lunch!

PATTY: That's very sweet, Jennifer, but you didn't tell me.

JENNIFER: Yes I did! I mean I think I did. I said I wanted to see you and how was twelve on Thursday?

PATTY: And I said I was delighted to see you at twelve-thirty?

JENNIFER: Or twelve and I asked if you liked Connolly's?

PATTY: And I said I did?

JENNIFER: Therefore . . .

PATTY: Is it me? I still don't hear the word *lunch.*

JENNIFER: It's lunchtime. I wanted to talk. I mentioned Connolly's. I assumed you'd know.

PATTY: You and Max make a lot of assumptions.

JENNIFER: Oh, God. This is the last thing I wanted. A misunderstanding. After all that's happened. Look, if we go right now . . .

PATTY: Do you honestly think I could just go? Please! Jennifer, my lunches are sacred. That's when I solicit contributions and build alliances and defend myself against the relentless attacks of my adversaries. That's just the way it is in the not-for-profit world. As much as I might like to, I don't think I can waste a lunch on you.

JENNIFER: I'm sorry I wasn't clear.

PATTY: Well, I've got a minute or two before I have to run. Certainly enough time to hear what's on your mind. Sit.

*(Jennifer sinks deeply into the soft chair. Patty takes the straight chair.)*

PATTY: *(Continuing.)* Well?

JENNIFER: I just thought, you and I, we're both involved with brothers who are close and we haven't ever really spent time together. The two of us. Together.

PATTY: No. We haven't. Do you think maybe there's a reason for that?

JENNIFER: I guess there probably is. What's the reason?

PATTY: Go on, please.

JENNIFER: Oh. Well, now that Max and I are getting married —

PATTY: You and Max are getting married?

JENNIFER: Yes. Didn't Barry tell you?

PATTY: No, he didn't.

JENNIFER: Oh. Well, the big news is, we are.

PATTY: Interesting.

JENNIFER: Thanks so much, that's very sweet, we're both just thrilled. Anyway, Patty, I really want to be friends.

PATTY: That's very nice, Jennifer.

JENNIFER: Oh, good! I've always respected you, my God, you're so important and successful — even though I don't know exactly what it is you do — and I've never felt very close to you — and that's not a criticism — but you have to admit there's been a gulf between us which now we can bridge if we're good friends.

PATTY: Jennifer?

JENNIFER: Or Jenny. Yes?

PATTY: Barry has his little circle of friends and I have quite a number of friends of my own, professional and personal, some dating back to childhood. And of course we've made lots of friends as a couple.

JENNIFER: Of course. Nice going.

PATTY: Thanks. What I'm saying is, friendship is important to me. And my time is at a premium. For me to take you on as a friend means someone else gets bumped.

JENNIFER: Oh, dear, I didn't mean for anyone to get bumped.

PATTY: Hey, that's just the way it is, but before I bring the hammer down on a good friend, which I'm happy to do, I need to know: What is it you offer me as a friend? *(Pause.)* That's not a rhetorical question.

JENNIFER: You want me to tell you what I offer as a friend?

PATTY: If you're serious about it, yes. I'd like to know so I can make an informed decision.

JENNIFER: Well, I think I'm loyal and compassionate. Whenever a friend gets robbed or loses a parent or a pet, you can bet I'm there with cards and candy and hand-holding, whatever they need. Once I even soul-kissed a girlfriend who was going through a transitional phase. You could talk to my friends, they'd give me the highest recommendations. I can be lots of fun.

PATTY: I'd certainly welcome discovering that side of you.

JENNIFER: Patty, we really don't know each other. There were traumatic events that shaped me. Did I ever tell you about the fire?

PATTY: Oh, my God.

JENNIFER: Thanks for your sympathy, it was just awful —

PATTY: No. I'm just very concerned about the invitations to our benefit. I need to think this through.

*(Long pause as Patty thinks.)*

JENNIFER: Should I . . . ?

PATTY: Please, Jennifer. I need to think.

*(Jennifer waits as Patty thinks. Blackout.)*

# Worldness
## Jenny Lyn Bader

*Dramatic*

Suzanne and Viv (twenties)

> *In this poignant scene, Suzanne, a no-nonsense woman in her twenties, has come to a jail to visit her sister Viv who has been arrested for staging an environmental protest.*

> *A jail visitation room. Viv sits behind the glass, waiting. Suzanne enters and sits across from her. She opens the speaking panel so Viv can hear her. She stares at Viv.*

SUZANNE: Oh lord. Look at you. *(She weeps. Her cell phone rings.)* Hold on. Hi. Could you stop forwarding my calls, please? I'm dealing with a friend's personal emergency?
*(Viv looks at Suzanne.)*
SUZANNE: Thanks. *(Hangs up.)* Sorry. This has been the day from hell. How are you?
VIV: I'm. Loving. Centered. You know, considering . . . this. *(Beat.)* I need your help with the bail.
*(Suzanne nods and stares at Viv across the glass.)*
SUZANNE: Why did you do it?
VIV: I wanted to — spread hope? To remind the world *of* the world and of Worldness. *(Beat.)* And I guess I've always wanted to stage a protest.
SUZANNE: Couldn't you have staged a normal protest? With people holding signs and shouting things?
VIV: This seemed like the best way to send the message.
SUZANNE: *(Skeptical.)* To move into a tree.
VIV: *(Nods.)* And I read a magazine article about this girl who moved into a tree in California, Julie Butterfly, and —

SUZANNE: Julia Butterfly Hill was not . . . close with anyone in the lumber business, as far as I know. Did you remember, during this tree-sit of yours, that I work in the lumber business?

VIV: It may've crossed my mind. *(Beat.)* How's Mom?

SUZANNE: She's a little upset. First you don't go into the family business — and now you go — sit in it.

VIV: I love Mom. Does she know how much I love the tree?

SUZANNE: Everyone in the Pacific Northwest knows how much you love the tree. You've got concerned citizens writing hate mail, religious activists saying logging is a sin. And you've even inspired a group of little girls to sit in trees in their backyards in your honor!

VIV: Really? I think it's so hard for kids to find someone to look up to. Or to have faith in any — You know, when we were little . . . *(She trails off.)*

SUZANNE: *(Irked.)* What? When we were little what?

VIV: *(Shakes her head.)* Nothing.

SUZANNE: When we were little, animals and plants loved you. Just like now. But I got along better than you with all of our relatives, living and dead. Always. You resent me. And this whole thing has not been for nature or the planet. It's been against me. And your phone call would never have been to me, except that you need money.

VIV: No! The phone call was . . .

SUZANNE: What about the money Grandpa left us? I invested mine. It's doubled.

VIV: I —

SUZANNE: Knowing you, you gave yours to those — tree people. Because you think that they are your family. And I will tell you now, I am your family. And they are tree people!

VIV: *(Genuinely upset.)* But Suzy I think of you as a tree person. Even when you cut them down. You're part of what I want to save. I wish I could save you.

SUZANNE: I wish I could save you! But you have to stop sitting in that tree. And get your friends out too.

VIV: What friends?

SUZANNE: You moved out, five of your friends moved in, with their own video cameras. You didn't see it on TV?

VIV: My friends were on TV? How great. Oh, not great. You're upset. You want me to . . . *(Realizes:)* Wait, I can't get them out if they have cameras! It would be taped! How ridiculous would I look!

SUZANNE: You? Have you considered how ridiculous I look?

VIV: No.

SUZANNE: I can just imagine my business school reunion now. "So, did you make your first hundred million by cashing out on your stock options?" — "No, I tried to make a living chopping down a few trees but I couldn't even do that because my sister was sitting in one of them!"

VIV: Angel. You shouldn't worry about what those people think . . .

SUZANNE: "And now to top it off, I have to bail her out of jail!"

VIV: Actually, if it makes you feel better, that money that Grandpa left us, I invested mine too.

SUZANNE: You did?

VIV: In a stock.

SUZANNE: Which stock?

VIV: Borzon.

SUZANNE: *(Stunned.)* You invested in an oil company?

VIV: I asked about environmentally responsible investing but the broker said that's for people with more money than I have.

SUZANNE: *(Moved.)* Viv, you had money in that bull market!

VIV: I'm selling it today, I just wanted to see if you would help me. If you would even visit. I miss you.

SUZANNE: Oh Viv. I thought you just wanted me . . . *(Interrupts herself.)* You really wanted to see me? *(Viv nods.)* But — you shouldn't sell Borzon now! It's a growth stock.

VIV: I realize that, but . . .

SUZANNE: Strategically, I'd advise you against it. Let me pay your bail. I want to.

VIV: *(Thrilled.)* You do? Oh thank you Suzy! *(Beat.)* I was going to say before, when we were little, you used to be my hero.

SUZANNE: Oh yeah? Who's your hero now?

VIV: I don't have one.

*(Suzanne nods in recognition.)*

SUZANNE: *(Beat.)* You know what? You're better off.

# Scenes for Men

# Diva
## Howard M. Gould

*Comic*

Isaac and Kurt (forties)

> *Isaac is the creator and head writer of a TV series starring a self-obsessed egomaniac named Deanna, who creates nothing but problems for him and for Kurt, the producer, with whom he is having a meeting in this scene.*

> *Isaac's office. Kurt sits on a sofa, Isaac opposite him in a guest chair.*

ISAAC: She eats through rehearsals. She fired two script supervisors last week alone. The second one bit the dust for correcting her when she called the actor "Ezra" on camera.

KURT: That's his name.

ISAAC: That's the *actor's* name. The character is "Jeremiah." Then she said we should change his character's name, make it easier for her to remember. In the second year of the show.

KURT: *(Laughs.)* Our Deanna.

ISAAC: Yeah. It's real cute. But not if you're the poor schmuck who got fired because this woman can't tell the difference between real life and television. You know what she's asking for now? This is why I had to talk to you.

KURT: I can't wait.

ISAAC: This week we're doing the episode about Deanna finding her birth mother? She calls me up yesterday — from her bathtub, no less — and tells me that America won't care about that. What America cares about, according to Deanna Denninger, is her hair.

KURT: Can't you just stick in a couple of hair jokes? I'm sure that would satisfy her.

ISAAC: Nope. Her shrink says it has to be the A-story.

KURT: Her shrink?

ISAAC: Oh, didn't I tell you? I do a notes session every week with one Dr. Kenneth Olshansky. Plus, believe it or not, I've had two script meetings with her nutritionist, and once I got three single-spaced pages from her animal psychic.

KURT: Animal psychic?

ISAAC: Yes, sir.

KURT: The psychic is an animal, or . . . ?

ISAAC: The psychic is a person, but he channels the souls of pets who've gone to the great kennel in the sky.

KURT: You've got your hands full.

ISAAC: She brought *her* dog to the writer's room. We were having dinner, and she put this little Pekinese on the table, so he could run around and sample everybody's Chinese food while she gave us notes on the script.

KURT: I can only hope that you're making this up.

ISAAC: I wish I were.

KURT: People have no idea how difficult television is, how the brutal hours and the nature of the schedule bring out the worst in everyone. In features, even if you have an extreme personality conflict, it's all over in a couple of months, and you simply go your separate ways and swear you'll never work together again. But TV — you're looking at years and years together, shackled at the ankle.

ISAAC: If you're lucky enough to have a hit.

KURT: I've never heard of a show that was easy. Not one. The writers hate the actors, the actors hate each other, everybody hates the network. There's always something. And it's eighteen hours a day, week after week, ten months a year.

ISAAC: *(Sighs.)* I think the only saving grace is that it keeps me away from an empty house.

KURT: I heard Meredith is moving up to Napa with the children.

ISAAC: Can't stop her. It's in-state. *(A beat, then:)* You know, you work eighty, ninety hours a week, there's nothing left for your family. Then comes the hiatus, and you've got two months to take your wife to Hawaii, ride bikes with your kids, get your life back. Two lousy months to remind yourself what it was all for in the first place. *(A deep breath.)* Then suddenly you hit that first hiatus *without* your family . . . and then you run into a season like *this*. . . *(A deep breath.)* If I had it all to do over . . . well, let's face it, I fucked up. *(A silence.)*

KURT: Look, I know it's a difficult time for you, and this is a particularly difficult show for many reasons. Just try as best you can to keep your cool until things settle down.

ISAAC: I'm not a prick, Kurt. It's not like I'm one of these asshole show-runners who tells the star just to say the lines and not bump into the furniture. But for the good of the show, we need her to focus on doing her job, and to let everyone else do theirs.

KURT: I understand. We'll talk to her when she gets here. I'm sure she'll be reasonable.

ISAAC: I just want what's best for the show.

KURT: As do I. That's why I put together this meeting.

ISAAC: Thank you.

# Diva
## Howard M. Gould

*Comic*

Barry (thirties to forties) amd Isaac (forties)

> *Isaac, the head writer and creator of a TV series starring a monstrously neurotically self-obsessed actress named Deanna, has come to his agent's office to discuss the problems he is having on the show in this scene, an outrageously witty satire of two show-biz creatures.*

BARRY: Isaac Brooks. *(Then.)* Emmy winner Isaac Brooks who spent last night schtupping America's sweetheart, Deanna Denninger.

ISAAC: *(Eyes still shut.)* Tell me when you're off the phone.

BARRY: I'm off. Asshole.

> *(Isaac finally looks at him.)*

BARRY: You really slept with her.

> *(Isaac grunts.)*

BARRY: Just be warned. That's a well-trodden path you journeyed, my friend.

ISAAC: Lovely metaphor.

BARRY: Just speaking the truth. The woman has her own little Vietnam down there. A lot of good men have gone, and not come back the same.

ISAAC: Look, I know how you have some issues with her.

BARRY: Issues? Not at all. In fact, I've been thinking I'd like to represent her. *(Off Isaac's look.)* What?

ISAAC: What do you mean, "what?" You? Represent *her?*

BARRY: You have to allow individuals credit for human growth. The better I get to know Deanna, the more I appreciate how things look from *her* perspective.

> *(Isaac looks at him in disbelief.)*

BARRY: Hey, she fired CAA and never signed anywhere else. I wanted to see how you feel about it, before I did anything, naturally.

ISAAC: Naturally.

BARRY: Stop looking at me like that. It's business.

ISAAC: But you're concerned about how I would feel. From the standpoint of the conflict.

BARRY: *(Waves it off.)* Conflict. There won't be a conflict . . .

ISAAC: Barry . . .

BARRY: You've got a hit show, and the two of you are a fabulous team. Even if, you know, the shared-limo thing doesn't entirely work out. Hey — you gave her back her career. She tells everybody that. I've never seen an actress so grateful.

ISAAC: I don't know, something about it makes me uneasy.

BARRY: Look, if I was even the least bit worried, I wouldn't bring this up. You and I have had situations in the past where you were hiring a writer I represented, or vice versa. Did we ever have a problem? And this'll be good for you, too.

ISAAC: Good for me?

BARRY: Two Emmys, the ratings'll get a nice bounce — sometime this year the network'll start talking extension. And *then* — you and Deanna negotiating together? Can you imagine how far we'll be able to ram it up Kurt's ass?

*(A silence.)*

BARRY: Look, as agents and clients go, I think we have something special.

ISAAC: I like to think so.

BARRY: You're not just any client to me, you're one of my closest friends.

ISAAC: And you're one of mine.

BARRY: If we do this, a time ever comes where there's a *hint* of conflict — *anything* — just say the word and I'll let her know she has to find someone else. You will always come first. Always.

ISAAC: Enough said. It's an opportunity. Go for it.

BARRY: You're sure.

ISAAC: And she couldn't ask for better. I'll tell her that myself.

BARRY: Would you? That'd be great. I'll follow your lead, you know, if that's OK. I don't want to push too hard with her.

ISAAC: When the time's right, plant a seed. I'll follow up.

BARRY: Plant a seed. Right. Not be too aggressive.

*(A silence.)*

ISAAC: I can't believe I really did that last night. It doesn't even seem real . . .

BARRY: Well . . . speaking as your agent, this could be a good thing. *(Off Isaac's look.)* Scandal gives you character. People want to know you, get into business with you. Elizabeth Hurley, most beautiful woman in the world, nobody gives a shit. Then her boyfriend gets a blowjob from a hooker with no teeth, boom, everybody wants to take a meeting.

ISAAC: It's a sick industry.

BARRY: Sick society. Remember Cosby, when his son got killed? People loved it. His ratings went through the roof. 'Course, out here, every-one's feeling bad for Bill, sending flowers. CBS even had a moment of silence on the air, you know, very tasteful . . . but believe me, next morning, when they saw that twenty-eight share, they were dancing in the fucking parking lot.

ISAAC: Barry — !

BARRY: What, are you going to *disagree* with that? Come on, you know that's how it works. So you're a family man, I respect that. I'm just saying, if you're screwing around anyway —

ISAAC: I'm not screwing around.

BARRY: Well, whatever you want to call last night, I'm just saying as a friend that I won't be judgmental, and, as your representative that, at the end of the day, there may actually be a professional upside.

ISAAC: Deanna's not a career tool, she's a *person*. A terrific person.
  *(A beat.)*

BARRY: Is this love? Shit man, don't tell me this is love.

ISAAC: It's not love. It was a stupid, one-night, too-much-champagne thing, and I'm kind of embarrassed about it, and I'd like it all to just go away before there's any real damage.

BARRY: Oh, man. She really rotated your tires, didn't she.

ISAAC: Stop it.

BARRY: Look at you. She really reupholstered your sofa.

ISAAC: Come on . . .

BARRY: She really de-boned your fish. *(Then:)* Deanna!

# Goldfinger's Army
## Brook Barry

*Comic*

Brian and Rickwall (twenties to thirties)

> *This outrageous farce takes place during the climactic moment in a new* Goldfinger *adventure. (Goldfinger's back, he didn't die, and Bond is off somewhere trying to foil him.) Brian is Goldfinger's accountant. He's a mild-mannered sort who took the job not knowing what he was getting into. Rickwall is a no-nonsense military type, one of Goldfinger's minions.*

> *Rickwall takes off his gloves and puts his hand out to Brian.*

RICKWALL: Rickwall. Lieutenant.
    *(Brian shakes the hand.)*
BRIAN: Brian Murray. Payroll.
RICKWALL: You told me.
BRIAN: I know.
RICKWALL: Where do you think the girl went?
BRIAN: Who knows? Maybe she zip-lined down the power lines.
RICKWALL: I don't think so.
BRIAN: Not like him. Did you see him? Holding on by a rubber phone cord! Zing! Sparks flying! Now that was cool.
RICKWALL: I never got a good shot at him.
BRIAN: He lands. People shooting lasers at him. Explosions everywhere. He buttons his dinner jacket and dives off the rocks. Buttons his dinner jacket. What's he gonna do? Visit the club on the way down?
RICKWALL: He'll never make the swim to the mainland. He probably didn't make it past the rocks.
BRIAN: Nice dive though.

RICKWALL: Either way, you saw the sharks on the way in. He's going to make it about thirty yards from here — then he's fish bait.

BRIAN: The sharks. My god.

RICKWALL: She's still around here, though. I can feel it. It's an animal thing. I can feel her breathing. I can feel her heart beating. I know she's around here. In my blood. You know what I'm talking about?

BRIAN: No no no. I'm married. I haven't felt anything like that for years.

RICKWALL: I mean combatwise.

BRIAN: Well, whatever. I don't feel her.

RICKWALL: I heard her scream. While the fighting was going on. And I knew who she was. Not her specifically. Who her type was.

BRIAN: A babe.

RICKWALL: Right.

BRIAN: A Double-OH babe.

RICKWALL: Yeah. As in double "Oh! YEAH!"

*(Brian giggles.)*

And I got this plan. This plan to get Goldfinger's whole operation in the free and clear. Came like a laser shot. Zap! I figured out a way to eliminate Goldfinger's main opposition and open the way for total world domination! And, just as suddenly, I knew I was the man to do it. Me. The man. I can't believe she got away.

BRIAN: It's not our job to come up with plans.

RICKWALL: It's not your job.

BRIAN: It's Goldfinger's job. We're just . . .

RICKWALL: Just what?

BRIAN: Lower-level employees.

RICKWALL: The forgettable! That's what we are! Extras. Background. Marching in formation. Standing too close to Thunderball. — BOOM! "AAAIIIEEEE!"

*(He throws himself onto the ground.)*

BRIAN: Don't even joke about that. Old man Warner lost an eye to Thunderball. He's in my barracks. He wakes up screaming obscenities at Jill St. John.

*(Rickwall sits up.)*

RICKWALL: That's not going to happen to me. I got a future. I'm gonna be a major plot point.

BRIAN: And I'm going to win the lottery.

RICKWALL: Thing big, be big, my friend.

*(He gets up and looks out the window.)*

BRIAN: I wish they would have mentioned the sharks in the brochure.

RICKWALL: So there's sharks. What of it?

BRIAN: You can't lie to your own people. He's gonna rule the world. I expected more.

RICKWALL: Yeah, well he had better things to do with his money than make a Club Med. Like these uniforms. Not cheap.

BRIAN: My helmet doesn't breathe. And it's heavy as a sink.

RICKWALL: What about the computers?

BRIAN: I don't even have a color monitor.

RICKWALL: The subjugation of the planet will not be deterred by the petty whining of the unenlightened!

*(He glares at Brian. Then he sits.)*

BRIAN: And my handset never works.

RICKWALL: Shut up.

# In Arabia
# We'd All Be Kings
## Stephen Adly Guirgis

*Dramatic*

Lenny (twenties to thirties) and Vic (probably older)

> *Lenny is a recently released ex-convict. Vic is interviewing Lenny about a possible job.*

> *Monday morning, 9:00 AM. An office on 37th Street.*

VIC: Siddown, Mr. . . .

LENNY: Lenny.

VIC: "Mr. Lenny," have a seat.

LENNY: Yes, sir . . .

VIC: . . . Sit . . . That's some cologne you're wearing.

LENNY: Thanks, uh, you want some?

VIC: I think you got us both covered there, Lenny. Quick question: You been drinkin'?

LENNY: Uh . . .

VIC: It's OK.

LENNY: Long night, but —

VIC: It's OK. If Vic says, "It's OK," then, "It's OK" . . . OK?

LENNY: Um . . .

VIC: Say, "OK."

LENNY: OK.

VIC: If we find you drinkin' on the job, you're out on your ass though, OK?

LENNY: I wouldn't do that —

VIC: So, Mr. Lenny, tell me: Why do you want to be an On-Site Field Engineer?

LENNY: Uh, I thought this job was for handin' out flyers.

VIC: It is.

LENNY: Oh.

VIC: But it's a lot more than that, Lenny. Lemme ask you somethin, Len: Where do you see yourself in five years?

LENNY: Thass a . . . I see myself . . . You know what I see, uh —

VIC: Lemme tell ya a little story, Len. Three years ago, I was right where you are now.

LENNY: Yeah?

VIC: Worse. Times are tough, right?

LENNY: A little.

VIC: Not for me, Len, not anymore, and I'll tell you why: They took my house, they took my wife, my kids, my car, all the creature comforts, you know what they didn't take? . . . Ask me what they didn't take!

LENNY: What —

VIC: My initiative, Len! A man with initiative, like yourself, like me, they can't take that away. Tell me the truth: You almost didn't come right?

LENNY: It's true.

VIC: But you did come. Hey! They can send me all the college grads and M.B.A.'s they want, you know what I say? I say, "Send me one man with initiative, I don't want "Yale," fuck Yale! Give me one guy: School a Hard Knocks and some fire in his eye." You got that fire, Len?

LENNY: I do.

VIC: 'Cuz if you don't, please, tell me now.

LENNY: Nah, I got it.

VIC: OK . . . The moustache, it goes. We like our Marketeers clean shaven.

LENNY: My moustache?

VIC: Policy . . . Now, hypothetical question: How many flyers you think you can hand out in ten hours?

LENNY: Uh, like a thousand?

VIC: Doesn't help me. You could hand out two thousand, three; you could toss half a them in a garbage —

LENNY: I wouldn't do that.

VIC: That's not the point. The point is: Can you get the people up here?

Can you get ten people per day to come up here, apply for a credit card?

LENNY: Credit card?

VIC: You wanna hand out Chinese takeout? That's across the street. You wanna make commissions? That's here. Every person you get up here, applies for a no-deposit, low-interest credit card, pays the fee, and gets accepted, that's five dollars in your pocket! Get ten people, that's fifty! Get twenty people, Len, you're lookin' at hundred a day, and that's on top of your regular three bucks an hour!

LENNY: Three bucks an hour!

VIC: After training, yeah. Now, here's a piece of paper. I want you to write down the name, address, and phone number of twenty of your friends and family, anybody you know who's got bad credit.

LENNY: For what?

VIC: Every name you give me, it's like you've handed out a flyer. Anybody you know buys a credit card from us, five dollars in your pocket.

LENNY: You know what? I would prefer to just hand out the flyers . . . With my moustache still on, if that's possible.

VIC: . . . I'm sorry to hear that. Tell you what, why don't you give me a call next week?

LENNY: No, no, you don't understand. I could hand out the flyers, I'm good at that.

VIC: I'm sure you are. Call me next week.

LENNY: OK, look, I'll shave the moustache, it's not a problem.

VIC: Like I said —

LENNY: I see how they hand out those flyers on the street, most a those guys, they don't do it right, I watch them —

VIC: Lenny, I got another appointment coming in.

LENNY: All right, why don't you just give me back my application fee, and I'll take off.

VIC: Nonrefundable.

LENNY: What?

VIC: Is this your signature?

LENNY: Hey! Juss gimme my fuckin' five dollahs back.

VIC: *(Into intercom.)* Ray? Get Rakim and Sal in here, we got a problem with an applicant.

LENNY: Who you think you playin' wit'? Gimme my fuckin' five dollahs! *(Rakim and Sal enter.)*

RAKIM: Problem?

LENNY: What is this, a mugging?

VIC: Show Lenny the lobby.

# Mickey Finn

## Mike Houlihan

*Comic*

Ray and Fitz (thirties to fifties)

> *This scene takes place in a bar, where Fitz and Ray, a bartender and a crooked cop, discuss whether or not to bump off a college professor who is having an affair with their pal Mickey's wife.*

> *Fitz is behind bar and Ray is standing at the bar, fidgeting. He's in uniform.*

RAY: How come you never got married?

FITZ: Elke Sommer and I didn't travel in the same circles.

RAY: You could've found yourself a nice Irish gal in the neighborhood who would've dragged you to the altar in a second.

FITZ: Yeah, it's the altar part that scares me. Isn't that where the sacrifice takes place?

RAY: What're you afraid of?

FITZ: Who said anything about bein' afraid?

RAY: Either that or you're a homo.

FITZ: Maybe I am. I don't know, I see all you happy couples out there, and I think about what a great husband I'd be, and how great it would be to coach my kid's Little League team with all the other dipshits, and bustin' my balls to pay a mortgage, tuition, and braces, and I think, ahh fuck it, who gives a shit. Yeah, I'm afraid.

RAY: Of what?

FITZ: Salvation.

RAY: What about it?

FITZ: I've got too many doubts. Takin' a vow is serious stuff. The flesh is willing but the spirit is weak.

RAY: Whattya mean?

FITZ: Just like you, I don't want burger every night. I like a place with a big menu.

RAY: And you don't have to send anything back, like a screachy burger.

FITZ: Ig fuckin' zackly! The other night I had this dream . . .

RAY: Yeah?

FITZ: Scared the shit out of me.

RAY: I never have dreams, not even nightmares.

FITZ: That's cuz your livin' one.

RAY: Not anymore I'm not. So what happened?

FITZ: I'm drivin' across one of the bridges downtown and the car crashes through and takes a dive right into the Chicago river. I'm thinkin' . . . "This is nothin', I can swim." But then I feel myself just bein' pulled down deeper 'n deeper. I'm sinkin' like a stone, "Well, I guess maybe this *is* it. Johnny Weismuller couldn't get out of this one."

RAY: Did your whole life flash before ya?

FITZ: Nah, I just started tryin' to figure out if I was gonna go to Heaven. OK, I'm ready to meet St. Pete. Will I get a good obit in the *Trib?* Where they gonna wake me? I'm thinkin', "Who gives a shit?" I'm sinkin' further n' further. I'm lookin' for the light everybody is talkin' about. What am I gonna say to him?

RAY: Yeah?

FITZ: And I find myself sayin', "Hey, I'm not ready."

RAY: Yeah, who *is?*

FITZ: That's exactly what he said.

RAY: Who?

FITZ: St. Peter.

RAY: *(As St. Pete.)* "You never really gave a shit for anybody but yourself."

FITZ: I know, I know I'm supposed to Pete, but hey, can't I enjoy this life a little without bein' a goo goo and carin' about every other asshole's spilt milk.

RAY: "Not all goo goo's get to Heaven."

FITZ: But Pete, what about those guys who do all sorts of evil shit, get caught, say they're sorry. And *then* they croak, like Dahmer?

RAY: "Dahmer, excuse me, but that guy was a fuckin' cannibal!"

FITZ: Yeah, but he at least got to *do* it — I haven't done half the evil shit that guy did and he's probably wearin' wings. Sure I wanna be saved, just not yet.

RAY: "You're just tryin' to save your ass."

FITZ: And everything connected to it, Pete.

RAY: *(As St. Pete.)* "Start thinkin' about savin' somebody else's ass and you just might save your own."

FITZ: You sound just like him!

RAY: Yeah, so then what'd he say?

FITZ: Nothin'.

RAY: Nothin'?

FITZ: No, that's when I woke up. In a cold sweat too, I might add.

RAY: So, you got a second chance.

FITZ: Yeah, that's the way I look at it too. So, it's a good thing I'm not married cuz I got a lot of evil shit to get done while I'm still on dry land.

RAY: You dipshit, that ain't what it means.

FITZ: So what's it mean, Sigmund?

RAY: It means you are a lowlife piece of shit who wants to do one decent thing in his pathetic life before he turns into a cannibal.

FITZ: One decent thing? What about all the fund-raisers I've thrown in this joint for busted-out cops, firemen, widows, and fuckin' orphans. You shittin' me, I'm practically the alderman in this neighborhood with all the freebies I've given out. And I've been plannin' that boxing night fund-raiser for Jimmy Goff's six fuckin' kids for almost a year.

RAY: OK, OK.

FITZ: Not to mention that benefit party we threw for you when you thought you were gettin' thrown off the force for police brutality.

RAY: Yeah, thanks I forgot.

FITZ: Shit I'll bet we raised over thirteen grand for your sorry ass, and then you go and get reinstated.

RAY: Only an idiot woulda given the money back.

FITZ: And what about my mother?

RAY: Your mother?

FITZ: I'm fuckin' devoted to her. I've been livin' in her fuckin' house my whole fuckin' life! Take her to Sportsmans Park six times a season,

Christmas, Easter, Thanksgiving, flowers every fuckin' birthday, which I haven't missed in forty-six years, Valentine's Day.

RAY: OK so you're a decent piece a shit, but havin' dreams about Dahmer means something is seriously wrong with your noodle.

FITZ: Oh thank you Dr. Laura Slushinger. I was just usin' Dahmer as an example. I mean Heaven is filled with jerks like him who copped a plea at the last minute, sought forgiveness and got saved, and then you got people like St. Theresa, who probably never cut a fart in public, sharin' the same Heaven with mopes like Dahmer.

RAY: I hope you weren't laying your salvation rap on Mickey, he's way beyond that now.

FITZ: What'd he say to you last night?

RAY: Nothin', what'd he tell *you?*

FITZ: He told me that a certain Hispanic doctor has been giving his old lady some very special injections.

RAY: What else?

FITZ: What else? Are you kiddin', the guy practically had a nervous breakdown in here tellin' me about some taco stealin' his wife.

RAY: Did he tell ya he wants to have this guy whacked?

FITZ: What?

RAY: *(Giggles.)* Nooooo, he didn't tell ya that did he?

FITZ: Are you shittin' me?

RAY: I shit you not, my friend. He offered me ten grand last night to whack this Mexican —

FITZ: Puerto Rican.

RAY: Same thing. Thousand Island or Russian.

FITZ: It ain't the same thing, there's a big difference, they get really pissed off if ya confuse 'em.

RAY: This Puerto Rican's gonna have a lot more to be pissed off about if Mickey follows through with his plan.

FITZ: He's got a plan? He's goofier than I fuckin' thought!

RAY: No shit.

FITZ: So what's his plan?

RAY: I just tole ya, he offered me ten grand to plug the guy.

FITZ: *That's* the plan? That's it? What'd he ask *you* for?

RAY: 'Cause I'm his friend hotshot, he trusts me . . . And because I got guns.

FITZ: That's a pretty horseshit plan. I mean, if I was gonna have somebody whacked . . . I wouldn't ask a Chicago cop to do it for me?

RAY: Why not, I've done it before.

FITZ: Please stop with the bullshit.

RAY: Maybe I never whacked anybody, but I've killed a few guys.

FITZ: Yeah, right, who did you ever kill?

RAY: I killed at least seven or eight gooks in Nam and I popped a Wilbur one night back in '75 over at Altgeld Gardens.

FITZ: What'd it feel like? Killing somebody.

RAY: It's no day at the beach.

FITZ: Oh it's gotta be a bad feelin'. But what kind of a bad feelin'?

RAY: Bad.

FITZ: Bad bad or really fuckin' bad?

RAY: Badder than the worst. Fuckin', fuckin', fuckin' bad. I thought I was gonna have a fuckin' heart attack with that kid in the Gardens. Broke out in a sweat, my heart is thumpin' like a fuckin' drum, almost passed out. The gooks were bad too, but fuck them, it was them or me. But this little shine comes out of the dark at me one night while we're investigatin' a shootin' over there and I swore I saw him lift his hand toward me as he's carrying heat. So I plugged him.

FITZ: Was it a gun?

RAY: No . . it wasn't.

FITZ: What was it?

RAY: A Baby Ruth.

FITZ: The kid was takin' a bite out of his candy bar and you smoked him?

RAY: Shut up Fitz. You don't know nothin' about it. The kid was dirty anyway, turns out later he *was* carrying a gun. Anyway, it's a bad feelin, when you suddenly see something you didn't expect. I had to go on leave for six months, thought I was gonna have a heart attack. *(Takes out pills and slugs it with beer.)* I'm still takin' pills for it.

FITZ: What kinda pills?

RAY: Pills.

FITZ: What kinda pills? Uppers? Downers? Murder pills, what?

RAY: Blood pressure pills, jagoff.

FITZ: They can't be heart pills, cuz you ain't got one. Not if you can pull a stunt like that.

RAY: I'd do it again if I had to.

FITZ: But this would be different.

RAY: No shit.

FITZ: Don't do it Ray. This would be premeditated murder.

RAY: Yeah, no surprises.

FITZ: So . . . what'd you tell Mickey?

RAY: Whattya think I tole him?

FITZ: I think you tole him that ten grand wasn't enough.

*(Blackout.)*

# More Lies About Jerzy

## Davey Holmes

*Seriocomic*

Jerzy and Arthur (forties)

> *This comic drama is a fictionalized imagining of the last days of the Polish novelist Jerzy Kozinski. In this scene, Jerzy and Arthur discuss an article Arthur has written about Jerzy.*

> *Doorbell. Lights up on Jerzy's apartment. Jerzy enters in his underwear, having just woken up. He shouts through the door.*

JERZY: Hello?

ARTHUR: Jerzy, it's Arthur. I should've called . . .

JERZY: Arthur Bausley?

ARTHUR: I wanted to talk —

JERZY: *(Throwing the door open.)* My friend!

> *(Arthur enters and notices Jerzy isn't dressed.)*

ARTHUR: I woke you up.

JERZY: It's a beautiful day and I would have missed it completely.

ARTHUR: I can come back . . .

JERZY: Good to see you.

> *(Jerzy startles Arthur by giving him a big hug.)*

JERZY: Your article was wonderful. A big success.

ARTHUR: Glad you think so.

> *(Jerzy makes a beeline for the bathroom.)*

JERZY: *(Exiting.)* I talked to one of the editors, Paul Ferryman, a good friend of mine —

ARTHUR: You know Mr. Ferryman?

JERZY: *(Offstage.)* He agrees that you have real talent!

ARTHUR: Thank you.

> *(We hear Jerzy pissing. Arthur immediately starts looking around; he*

*pokes his head into the kitchen, doubles back and moves toward the bedroom.)*

JERZY: They're hiring another critic soon. You're at the top of their list!

ARTHUR: *(Stops.)* I am?

*(The toilet flushes. Jerzy enters and begins gathering up various items of his clothing that lie scattered around the room.)*

JERZY: Pardon me while I straighten up.

ARTHUR: Was there anything about the article that bothered you?

JERZY: No, I thought it was —

ARTHUR: There must have been something.

JERZY: *(Pause.)* Well.

ARTHUR: What?

JERZY: *(Putting on his shirt.)* It's such a small . . .

ARTHUR: Please.

JERZY: Your job is to present facts in some sort of coherent order so people can form their own opinion of . . . whatever you're writing about. And you're careful how you do this. Very careful.

ARTHUR: You think I'm . . .

JERZY: A little dry.

ARTHUR: Oh.

JERZY: Which is not always bad. As a reader I trust you, you reek of objectivity. But . . . Lesnewski, born here, did that . . . There was room for more mystery. You can avoid imposing an opinion and still leave a taste of something drifting in the air . . .

ARTHUR: Of . . . ?

JERZY: Inference. No . . . *(Pauses with one pant leg on.)* Possibility. The details are there for their own sake, fine, or they are arranged as a question mark. Because life is possibility.

ARTHUR: I'm not sure I . . .

JERZY: A woman is standing fifty feet away, a stranger, you can't see her face. Next thing you know, you're using both fists to wash her menstrual blood out of your sheets. What does it mean?

ARTHUR: I don't know.

JERZY: Exactly! There are no words for it. And maybe there is more to your subject, in this case me, than can be conveyed with a fact. *(Then.)* The article is fine, it's a small point . . .

ARTHUR: I'm worried it wasn't dry enough.

(*Jerzy looks at him.*)

ARTHUR: You've read my reviews. I'm a fan. I was one of the first.

JERZY: I am indebted to you —

ARTHUR: But you're aware some of the dates you gave me conflict with your biography.

JERZY: Ryson is dyslexic. He almost misspelled my name on the —

ARTHUR: My research assistant assured me it was the biography which was incorrect. That you hadn't even seen the bio until it was published.

JERZY: That's right. I was furious.

ARTHUR: Ryson claims he gave you the manuscript. And that you made changes.

JERZY: He said . . .

ARTHUR: Many changes.

JERZY: Mm. (*Pause.*) I got it wrong then or now — I don't know, one or the other, does it matter? The exact date. The reference point for, what, something that happened to me . . .

ARTHUR: You didn't tell me you're in arbitration with the Authors Guild.

JERZY: Do you care?

ARTHUR: I do.

JERZY: Why? A proofreader claims, and how this would happen I'm not sure, that I tricked him into writing my book and took credit. Or something like that.

ARTHUR: So you arranged for an interview with a journalist who's gone on record as a fan —

JERZY: It wasn't that mercenary. It was an interview. I sat with you and tried to conjure a stream of lurid detail, my life. An unsound element or two flew past. I didn't notice, it wasn't important —

ARTHUR: But it is! To me it's very important. That everything be factual.

JERZY: Yes. I apologize.

(*A beat.*)

ARTHUR: Your book is, it's stunning. I hate to annoy you with this sort of —

JERZY: What else?

ARTHUR: (*Hesitates.*) My research assistant. Her name is Georgia. She assured me she'd straightened it out. I've worked with her before, she's usually very thorough and . . . Are you sleeping with her?

*(Jerzy is startled.)*

JERZY: Am I . . .? What makes you think we've even met?

ARTHUR: I don't know you well enough to be . . . prying into your . . . I hope you're not offended. It's just, there were indications.

JERZY: Are you serious?

ARTHUR: I should never have brought it up . . .

JERZY: You're dating this woman?

ARTHUR: No.

JERZY: In love with her.

ARTHUR: No, no, I'm . . . I respect her. I mean I like her, but it's a friendly . . . *(Then.)* So you're not sleeping with her?

JERZY: I'm not.

ARTHUR: I can't believe I . . . Forgive me.

JERZY: Well now I'm interested. Maybe you could introduce us?

*(Their laughter is cut short as Georgia enters from the bedroom.)*

JERZY: That's it, wait until you hear me lie, then come out. *(Then.)* I'm making coffee. Would either of you . . . ?

ARTHUR: Yes, please.

*(Jerzy exits.)*

# Saints at the Rave

## Guillermo Reyes

*Comic*

Roommate and Saint (late teens)

> *This comedy takes place in a college dorm room at a Catholic school. A young student (Roommate) has prayed for guidance from St. Augustine, when who should show up but the saint himself; only, not the saintly theologian but the young reprobate he was before he found God's grace. In other words, this Augustine is now this student's roommate from Hell.*

> *A college dorm, modern times. The Roommate enters and sees St. Augustine sleeping on the couch.*

ROOMMATE: All right, get up.

SAINT: Huh?

ROOMMATE: Your bags are ready, and the Carmelite nuns have agreed to put you up until you can be sent back to — to, you know, the fourth century or wherever it is you belong.

SAINT: Oh? Huh?

ROOMMATE: I'm sorry, St. Augustine, but this exchange program just isn't working out anymore. Your behavior's been lewd, gross, and a bit too Ancient Rome for my taste. I was expecting a lot more from you and . . . well, have you anything to say for yourself?

SAINT: *(Burping.)* Arrrgh!

ROOMMATE: Oh, that's good, that's really good. Maybe it's my fault. I thought you'd be good at least for research.

SAINT: To you, I was just research?

ROOMMATE: Well, frankly, yes, but — wait, why am I feeling apologetic? You're the one who stayed up all night at the rave doing mushrooms — or was it Ecstasy? Don't answer that! I really wish you would just pick up and go now, and consider this exchange a bad experiment in intercentury activities.

SAINT: You didn't specify.

ROOMMATE: What?

SAINT: Dude, when you asked for St. Augustine of Hippo, you didn't specify the older, wiser scholar. They sent you the young debaucher instead! You can order St. Augustine in all of life's passages.

ROOMMATE: Spare me the Gail Sheehy analysis. Your bags are packed.

SAINT: Well . . . geez . . . man, oh, man, I'm sorry —

ROOMMATE: No need to apologize. I fooled myself. I forgot that besides being a saint, you were also a man.

SAINT: "Man." You say it with such disdain.

ROOMMATE: After all, this is a Catholic college. I thought I'd left all that teenage excess behind in high school, but no, this lack of discipline among my contemporaries, it's quite overwhelming! You should go now!

SAINT: All right, I will!

ROOMMATE: Wait! I mean no — just go, go!

SAINT: I am —

ROOMMATE: Wait! *(Roommate starts to cry.)*

SAINT: Now, what's this?

ROOMMATE: Never you mind.

SAINT: Say it.

ROOMMATE: When you first came, you were like a brother, you know.

SAINT: Yeh?

ROOMMATE: You explained the Manichean heresy so well, I got an A in that exam. I've never had a brother, you know, not a sister, nor anybody who could be wiser than I am.

SAINT: It's good to have a saint around, yeh.

ROOMMATE: I thought so.

SAINT: You wanna go raid the pear orchard?

ROOMMATE: What? Now why do you do that?

SAINT: I don't know, it's a prank, builds comradeship amongst pranksters.

ROOMMATE: As President of Catholic Youth, I'm deeply offended by your behavior.

SAINT: Well, you know what, Mr. President of Catholic Youth? I'm a little tired myself of you cloaking yourself in my religion, the one I helped define, to judge me! Me! I reached my state of beatitude the hard way, dude! I had to struggle with lust, and gluttony and — you know the other deadly sins —

ROOMMATE: You mean you don't know the seven deadly si —

SAINT: I said don't judge me! I didn't become the saint without struggling with those sins in the fourth century the way you are in the twenty-first.

ROOMMATE: I've done well against sin!

SAINT: The point is you wanted me to be an example and I only ended up a man who has to undergo his life's passages like any other. I'm sorry if you don't want me around — I could have used your help.

ROOMMATE: My help?

SAINT: Sure, I never had anybody to confide in either. Somebody to help me steer away from sin, you know.

ROOMMATE: This is the vulnerable stage of your life passage, isn't it?

SAINT: The most vulnerable.

ROOMMATE: We could pray for you, I suppose.

SAINT: That, too, but how about learning to just . . . listen.

ROOMMATE: To you? I mean . . . all right, all right, I see . . . you need a friend.

SAINT: Good, you're helping me, see? Helping me steer away from sin which is something St. Augustine really needed at this age.

ROOMMATE: Well . . . I suppose I can do that, but don't push your luck —

SAINT: If I misbehave, if I fall into temptation, I'm sure you'll be there to remind me.

ROOMMATE: Would you also take your socks and put them in the laundry basket or something?

SAINT: Sure. We could go do laundry, and then make some of that hangover soup —

ROOMMATE: Too first century, just take Tylenol.

We could go to dinner though —

SAINT: The steak house —

ROOMMATE: All right, the steak house —

SAINT: I know some Puerto Rican girls who work there who are dyyyying to meet you —

ROOMMATE: No allusions to Mick Jagger, please —

SAINT: Sorry!

ROOMMATE: We'll buy you Gregorian chants. You'll see, Saint Augustine, I'll help you steer away from sin.

SAINT: Sure you will. Brothers?

ROOMMATE: All right . . . brothers.

# Thief River
## Lee Blessing

*Dramatic*

Ray and Gil (thirties to forties)

> *This drama is the story of Ray and Gil, two gay men who were lovers in their twenties. We watch their lives intersect at three different ages — two young men, two middle-aged men, and two old men — so Ray and Gil are played by six different actors. This scene is between Ray 2 and Gil 2, middle-aged men who used to be lovers; but now Ray is married with children. They haven't seen each other in a while, and in this scene they discuss whether or not to rekindle their love.*

> *1973. Ray 2 looks out the window. Gil 2 kneels on all fours, examining the floor.*

RAY 2: Look at Perry with that horrible little kid of yours. What on earth you think they're talking about?

GIL 2: Kit's very well-read in certain areas. What's Perry know about lingerie?

RAY 2: If they're talking flannel, everything. Perry can sit and listen to anybody about anything. Listens to all sides, too. That's pretty rare up here — well, you know. Doesn't always tip his hand, either. It was three years before I knew what he thought of me and Molly getting married.

GIL 2: Maybe we should've died here. Like a pair of great lovers.
I can still see my blood, I think.

RAY 2: *(Still looking out the window.)* Most patient man I know.

GIL 2: Who?

RAY 2: Perry. Haven't you been listening?

GIL 2: Haven't you?

RAY 2: I can see why you want to be with me. It's like we're married already.

GIL 2: Like we always have been. *(As Ray 2 turns away.)* We'd be such a great couple. We wouldn't have to live in Brooklyn Center. I wouldn't make you do that.

RAY 2: We sure couldn't live here.

GIL 2: We'd go to New York; we'd both be lost. We'd be this aging gay couple, holding hands on the sidewalk, no matter how corny it looked — except at night, when the kids from Jersey with the baseball bats show up.

RAY 2: Where did you get all this?

GIL 2: I read.

RAY 2: Believe me, you're making New York sound *real* attractive.

GIL 2: It is! You can say, "I'm gay," and — in general — they won't kill you. They really won't.

*(Ray gives him a rueful smile.)*

RAY 2: Not many farms in Manhattan.

GIL 2: There are one or two fine parcels of land left in the Village. They're perhaps a bit smaller than what you have here —

RAY 2: It'd be tough to get by on anything smaller.

GIL 2: We'll supplement. I'll take in laundry.

RAY 2: How'm I going to get the heavy equipment there?

GIL 2: Drive?

RAY 2: Down the freeway?

GIL 2: On the shoulder. No problem's too big.

RAY 2: Guess not. Where'll I put all my personal things?

GIL 2: Personal things?

RAY 2: You know — wife, son . . .

*(Gil goes silent. If he's on the floor, he rises.)*

GIL 2: Trunk. Open it up once a year on Christmas.

RAY 2: Doesn't sound too fair —

GIL 2: *I was there first.*

RAY 2: No, you weren't. I was going with Molly —

GIL 2: *(Poking Ray 2 gently on the chest.)* I was there. First. *(A beat.)* Why'd you stop writing to me?

RAY 2: My son's getting married.

GIL 2: So?

RAY 2: Twenty-five years. What was I doing? Who I was doing it for? I didn't know anymore. I couldn't . . . Nobody can live on that, Gil. It's a ghost. *(After a beat.)* Besides, I have to be a family man. I have to be for them, or I'm not . . . for them.

GIL 2: Hard to be articulate when you don't believe what you're saying.

RAY 2: I don't expect you to understand —

GIL 2: Why? 'Cause I didn't make a fake family?

RAY 2: *It's not fake!*

GIL 2: You are. Every week, when you write that letter, you are fake. No, I take that back. That's the one time you are genuine.

RAY 2: What we had was over a long time ago —

GIL 2: It's not over. You know, maybe I wish it was over too, but it isn't.

RAY 2: Gil —

GIL 2: If it was over, you'd have shoved Kit and me back in our car and told us to get the hell out. But you didn't. Look where we are, Ray. Look where we're standing.

RAY 2: *(Turning away from him.)* You know the kind of questions that are going through my family's minds right now?

GIL 2: I'm sorry.

RAY 2: You destroyed that rehearsal. I suppose I'm lucky you didn't stumble in here tomorrow and ruin the real thing.

GIL 2: I don't pretend I know what I'm doing here. Any more than you know — really — why you stopped writing. All I know is that I have questions. About us. I need the answers. You know, it's totally different out there. The way we grew up . . . here . . . you're right, we probably couldn't have done it, but now . . . I can be a person out there. So can you. And it's only going to get better —

RAY 2: You're with Kit.

GIL 2: And you're with Molly, but I don't see them here.

RAY 2: I can't rip up everyone's life around me.

GIL 2: You're better off lying to them?

RAY 2: *Why not?* It was better to lie. She earned that lie. All she's ever done is love me. *(A beat.)* I won't leave them. I won't leave my son.

GIL 2: He's a grown man. He's getting married. Besides, he hates people like us.

RAY 2: Ray Junior's his own person — all right? I mean, you walk in unannounced with that . . . that creature —

GIL 2: He's not a "creature" —

RAY 2: My son's never seen anybody like that, he's never been around —

GIL 2: And that gives him the right to throw Kit over a pew? What the hell kind of values did he grow up with, Ray?

RAY 2: *Our* values! This town's values! I did what I could, I told him everyone's a human being; that doesn't mean he has to listen to me. He's got his own mind. I can't change that — I *wouldn't* change it. Why in hell did you bring Kit in the first place!?

GIL 2: I didn't want to. He insisted. He lives with me, Ray. You think I can hide how I feel? He's jealous, and he's just trying to fuck everything up in his own, adorable little way.

RAY 2: And he doesn't matter to you?

GIL 2: I don't know. That's what I'm saying. That's why I'm here. I want to find out, I want to *know*, if you and I can —

RAY 2: We can't. *(After a beat.)* We won't. You and Kit get in your car. Get out of here. *(As Ray 2 starts for the front door, Gil 2 sits down on the floor. Ray 2 looks back.)* Gil —

GIL 2: God sees us, Ray.

RAY 2: Will you get up? *(Instead, Gil 2 lies on his back, staring up.)*

GIL 2: God sees us.

RAY 2: When did you get religion?

GIL 2: I didn't. But God sees what He made. I don't need religion to know that. *(Holding his hand above him, studying it.)* My body is religion. Each cell. What I know in each cell. It's all we are: billions — trillions? — of cells. Each one with a wall. Each and every one. Trillions of walls. That's what we're mostly made up of: walls.

RAY 2: Some of us are mostly made up of horseshit.

GIL 2: But which ones? *(After a beat.)* Say you don't love me. Say it. I'll go. *(A silence.)*

RAY 2: Some nights, when Molly's asleep — in the same room, in the same bed where you and I first . . . I'll get up, and . . . I'll go downstairs. I have to walk way on the far edges of the steps so they don't creak, and . . . eventually I'll get downstairs. And I'll see the living room. You remember that day in the living room.

GIL 2: Yes.

RAY 2: And if it's summer I'll go out on the porch. And I'll just sit there on the rail, where we sat. That night you first held my hand. In the dark. For an hour. *(A beat.)* And then I'll go back upstairs to bed. Some nights, I can even fall asleep again. *(A beat.)* In the morning, Molly's always so pretty. Always so rested. She has so much energy.

GIL 2: Molly's a strong woman.

RAY 2: She is.

GIL 2: She'd survive losing you.

RAY 2: *(Turning away from him.)* You don't know a thing about it. I married her. We had a son. That's it — that's my life. I take care of them.

GIL 2: You also take care of an abandoned house. *(After a beat.)* What if it comes out?

RAY 2: What?

GIL 2: You and me.

RAY 2: It's not going to come out —

GIL 2: I could make it come out.

RAY 2: If you did that, you'd never hear from me again.

GIL 2: What have I got to lose?

RAY 2: She'd never believe you.

GIL 2: I have your letters, Ray. I brought them with me. Boxes and boxes.

RAY 2: You didn't.

# When the Sea Drowns in Sand*

## Eduardo Machado

*Dramatic*

Federico and Fred

> *This drama is about a gay man of Cuban ancestry who travels to Havana to discover his roots. He has brought along a friend named Federico, who is also on something of a voyage of self-discovery to decide if, in fact, he is Fred's lover.*

FEDERICO: Son of a bitch called me a tourist.

FRED: You feel like a woman?

FEDERICO: What?

FRED: You said that you feel like a woman. You said she flew then fell. No pride . . .

FEDERICO: Yes, so what!

FRED: I feel like a woman. I'm not gay, but I feel like a woman.

FEDERICO: Two girls lost in La Habana?

FRED: What?

FEDERICO: You and I. Two girls lost in La Habana. *(Imitates Blanche.)* Did you take a car down El Malecon, through a tunnel, to a town called Cojimar . . .

FRED: Stop it!

FEDERICO: Come on, do Blanche for me. Are you Blanche inside that macho body? Does Blanche really dwell inside your soul?

FRED: Stop it! Don't make fun of me.

*(Fred sulks.)*

FEDERICO: Jesus, Fred?

---

*Produced in New York City as *Havana Is Waiting*.

FRED: I tell you something about myself . . .

FEDERICO: Oh.

FRED: Something fragile inside of me and you exploit it.

FEDERICO: Sorry, I don't like it when you talk that bullshit.

FRED: "Talk that bullshit"! My insides are bullshit to you!

FEDERICO: No . . . But that girl stuff . . . when you finger a dress, or put on a little lipstick . . . And that time you went through Natasha's closet and tried on her dresses and modeled.

FRED: Let me tell you something! I fucked Natasha good and hard that night. Yeah! Good and hard!

FEDERICO: Really?

FRED: Yeah gave it to her. Gave it . . .

FEDERICO: I believe you.

FRED: All night long, baby. I left her begging for more. Yeah.

FEDERICO: Please stop talking like that!

FRED: Like what?

FEDERICO: Like a fifties man.

FRED: Fifties man and nineties chick. What a combination. What the fuck? Jesus, what a mess.

*(Fred starts to cry.)*

FEDERICO: Fred don't. Don't you dare fall apart on me.

FRED: I once looked in the mirror at my face and I saw a line going up and down, dividing my face . . . the line went all the way down my body one side masculine the other feminine. I could not move for hours it was all too clear. I felt so weak. Divided, I don't know where to run. Split. And it scares the shit out of me. Hold me!

FEDERICO: Hold you?

FRED: Yes. Hold me.

FEDERICO: Hold you?

FRED: Yes, please!

FEDERICO: Well . . . no . . . I don't want to hold you. I don't want to hold a man on the block where I come from. Not here.

FRED: Look beyond my manly body. See the girl that needs you.

*(Fred cries.)*

FEDERICO: I'm frozen.

FRED: Please.

FEDERICO: I'm angry!

FRED: That I need you?

FEDERICO: That you'll use me.

FRED: No, that I need you!

FEDERICO: That you'll ask me to open up every part of me. My heart, my brain, my nipples, my thighs, my testicles, my penis . . . And then you'll tell me . . . "What do you think I am?"

FRED: You know I'm straight.

FEDERICO: You are not at this moment.

FRED: What?

FEDERICO: You are not straight at this moment.

FRED: No. At this moment . . . I need a man . . . I need you. Please. Look at me I'm not hiding anything.

FEDERICO: No, you're not.

FRED: No. This is me.

FEDERICO: I . . . am . . . walking toward you . . .

*(They embrace. They touch each other. They kiss each other's necks. They look into each other's eyes.)*

FRED: We just held each other.

FEDERICO: I know.

FRED: Yes.

FEDERICO: Yes.

FRED: Don't stop.

FEDERICO: All right.

FRED: We are holding each other.

FEDERICO: Like lovers.

FRED: I kissed your neck.

FEDERICO: I kissed yours.

*(They kiss each other's necks again.)*

FEDERICO: You grabbed my ass.

FRED: Yeah!

FEDERICO: We are looking into each other's eyes.

FRED: Take me in.

FEDERICO: If I take you in . . . if I take you in . . . we'd be lovers.

FRED: Maybe. Maybe not.

FEDERICO: No.

*(Federico closes his eyes.)*

FRED: Open them. Open your eyes!

FEDERICO: I can't.

FRED: In them I feel whole.

*(Frederico opens his eyes.)*

FRED: Thank you.

FEDERICO: Sure.

FRED: See everything?

FEDERICO: Yes.

FRED: You are a very needy person. So am I.

FEDERICO: Yes.

FRED: My friend.

FEDERICO: What?

*(Fred kisses Federico on the mouth. Federico pulls away.)*

FRED: No.

FEDERICO: My mouth opened.

FRED: I can forgive you.

FEDERICO: My bambino. My beautiful bambino.

FRED: My grandfather —

FEDERICO: Used to call you that.

FRED: Yes.

*(Fred buries his face on Federico's chest.)*

FEDERICO: If I had milk I'd suckle you.

FRED: You are suckling me.

FEDERICO: What a mess.

FRED: I'm not some nice stranger.

FEDERICO: You never were.

*(They hold each other.)*

FRED: Is anybody looking at us.

FEDERICO: Someone is always looking at us.

FRED: Who gives a fuck.

FEDERICO: *(Sings.)* "Hey there Georgy girl. There's another Georgy deep inside." "In-betweens we are just lonely in-betweens."

FRED: Not lonely. *(Sings.)* "Me and my shadow, all alone and feeling blue."

FEDERICO: "And when it's two o'clock, I climb the stairs,"

*(They dance.)*

FRED: "We never knock,"

FRED AND FEDERICO: " 'Cause nobody's there. Just me and my shadow, all alone."

FRED: Not alone.

FEDERICO: And feeling fine.

FRED: I want to be a man. But not a stereotype like my dad. "Where are the broads. She's got great tits, but she's a little bottom-heavy. Want to get it in. You're getting too emotional, honey. You gotta cut me loose." I hate it when I say shit like that. I sound just like him.

FEDERICO: Yes.

FRED: A man who can love like a woman. That's what I want to be. That's what this country is bringing out in me.

FEDERICO: Every girl's ideal.

FRED: You think?

FEDERICO: Get Ernesto. Let's get out of here. I've been inside of you. Emotionally, I mean.

FRED: You can get inside of my emotions whenever you want.

FEDERICO: And inside of you, Fred, it's very warm and reassuring. I don't need to see the inside of that fucking house! Get him!

# Wonderful World
## Richard Dresser

*Comic*

Max and Barry (thirties to forties)

> *In this scene, Max and Barry, two brothers, meet in a bar to discuss what to do about the women in their lives.*

> *Lights up on a bar. Barry is sitting morosely at a little table with two huge empty mugs. Max enters with a small pitcher of beer, which he pours into the two mugs. The brothers watch like hawks to make sure it's equal. Neither gets much.*

BARRY: Jennifer came back?

MAX: Thank God for that freezing rain. She stumbled back in, drenched and sobbing.

BARRY: Good. Marriage is everything
*(They drink.)*

MAX: Are you two OK?

BARRY: Basically. Except Patty keeps leaving these mean little Post-its around the house for me to find. See?
*(Barry shows Max a few of the Post-its.)*

MAX: Wow. That *is* mean.

BARRY: I'll find these stuck on the refrigerator, the bathroom mirror, on my shoes in the morning. Gets the day off to a roaring start, let me tell you. I guess I shouldn't have told her what you and Jennifer said about her.

MAX: You told her? Why would you tell her?

BARRY: Patty has this power. She looks at me and I just panic. Do you know what a curse it is to suddenly find yourself telling the truth? Turns out on top of everything else she was mad I went to your house.

MAX: She wanted you to go. Didn't she?

BARRY: True. But she changed her mind after I left. I guess I should have seen that coming.

MAX: You should have known Patty was going to change her mind after you left?

BARRY: That's what she thinks. And the way she explains it, I believe her. The situation is worse that I thought, Max. I need your help.

MAX: You got it, Barry. Whatever you want.

BARRY: She's making slow but steady progress out of her funk. As a matter of fact, she is well enough to put pen to paper. This is a statement she released.

MAX: She released a statement?

BARRY: *(Gets out a paper.)* She writes, "My rage at your appalling cruelty in excluding me for dinner is slowly running its course. According to Barry, it was an 'oversight' rather than the craven act of heartless malice it would appear to be. Taking Barry at his word, I suppose I should feel encouraged to learn that you are simply stunningly selfish rather than aggressively evil."

MAX: She thinks I'm evil?

BARRY: No, she did but now she thinks you're just "stunningly selfish." See, if we analyze this, I think there's real cause for hope. I believe she's almost ready to receive your apology.

MAX: What exactly am I apologizing for?

BARRY: For excluding her from your dinner party. And for the terrible things you and Jennifer said about her.

MAX: I didn't exclude her. And I didn't even say anything bad. Jennifer, on the other hand, was on a senseless bloody rampage.

BARRY: But Patty knows what was said. She can't stop thinking about it. The pain goes on and on, Max. And it's your fault.

MAX: Why are you doing this? You don't have to do this.

BARRY: It's my duty to defend Patty's honor. Which you and Jennifer have besmirched. Although, frankly, we don't hold Jennifer as responsible as you.

MAX: Why not? She said much worse stuff than I did!

BARRY: Yes, but well, with Jennifer it's understandable.

MAX: Why?

BARRY: You know. Jennifer's a little flighty. Self-esteem issues. It's no wonder Patty intimidates her.

MAX: That's pretty insulting.

BARRY: Please. I love Jennifer. But, as Patty says, Jennifer blends right in with the furniture. One of these days someone's liable to just sit on her.

MAX: Patty said that?

BARRY: You know Patty, She's nothing if not honest. Bless her heart.

MAX: Maybe Jennifer was just being honest about Patty. Just the way Patty was being honest about Jennifer.

BARRY: Forget Jennifer. Jennifer's not the man. You're the man. So be the man and apologize and get it over with.

MAX: Do you know what I think? I think Patty should apologize to me for ruining our party.

BARRY: Are you serious?

MAX: Dead.

BARRY: Get real. It doesn't work that way.

MAX: What way?

BARRY: Can I trust you, Max?

MAX: Totally.

BARRY: Patty doesn't apologize.

MAX: Why not?

BARRY: She has many wonderful qualities, but in all the years we've been together, she's never once admitted she was wrong. I don't think she'll start now.

MAX: So you always have to be the one to apologize?

BARRY: If I didn't our fights would never end.

MAX: Jesus Christ. How do you stand it?

BARRY: Because she's so great in every other way. It's just this one thing she can't do. We all have stuff we can't do. I can't fly an airplane, for example.

MAX: That shouldn't cripple your marriage.

BARRY: For example! That's why you've got to help me. You've got to reach out to Patty.

MAX: Or what?

BARRY: Or you and I are through.

MAX: We're not going to be brothers anymore? How will we do that? Travel back in time and kill our parents?

BARRY: I can't fraternize with you and then go home to Patty. She considers you the enemy.

MAX: Do you think I'm the enemy, Barry?

BARRY: I took vows. Big scary vows. My marriage depends on this. Don't make me choose between you and Patty, because Patty will frankly kick your ass.

MAX: You're not giving me any wiggle room, Barry.

BARRY: Look at me. Max. Does it look as if I have any wiggle room? I know for a fact that Patty doesn't have any wiggle room either. Nobody has any wiggle room because you have insulted her honor. Until you apologize to Patty, you aren't my brother.

*(Barry downs his beer and leaves. Blackout.)*

196